# GREAT
## EXPLORERS

# OXFORD

UNIVERSITY PRESS

Great Clarendon Street, Oxford OX2 6DP

Oxford University Press is a department of the University of Oxford.
It furthers the University's objective of excellence in research, scholarship,
and education by publishing worldwide in

Oxford   New York

Auckland   Cape Town   Dar es Salaam   Hong Kong   Karachi
Kuala Lumpur   Madrid   Melbourne   Mexico City   Nairobi
New Delhi   Shanghai   Taipei   Toronto

With offices in

Argentina   Austria   Brazil   Chile   Czech Republic   France   Greece
Guatemala   Hungary   Italy   Japan   Poland   Portugal   Singapore
South Korea   Switzerland   Thailand   Turkey   Ukraine   Vietnam

Oxford is a registered trade mark of Oxford University Press
in the UK and in certain other countries

British Library Cataloguing in Publication Data

Data available

ISBN: 978-0-19-911678-2

Originated and created for Oxford University Press
by the Brown Reference Group

1 3 5 7 9 10 8 6 4 2

Printed in China

# GREAT EXPLORERS

Jim Pipe

Discovering the World

OXFORD
UNIVERSITY PRESS

# TABLE OF CONTENTS

# WHY EXPLORE?

HUMANS ARE BORN EXPLORERS. WE WANT TO KNOW WHAT IS 'OUT THERE' FOR OURSELVES. IN THE PAST, THIS IMPULSE SPURRED BRAVE MEN AND WOMEN TO THE ENDS OF THE EARTH. TODAY, IT SENDS ASTRONAUTS INTO SPACE AND SCIENTISTS TO THE OCEAN DEPTHS.

Over 30,000 years ago, Stone Age hunters followed migrating animals across the continents. Later, people looked for new places to barter goods or find valuable items such as gold or spices. Kings sent out raiding parties to look for lands to conquer.

The great 'Age of Discovery' began during the 15th century, when European mariners such as Columbus and Magellan set off in search of trading routes and new lands. By the end of the 20th century, most of the Earth's surface had been explored. Today's explorers look for new challenges in the deep ocean and in space.

The map of the world today is the result of hundreds of years of exploration.

In many cases, travellers were 'exploring' lands where other people already lived.

▼ In the 15th century, early explorers were at the mercy of wind and water as they sailed the seas in their galleons. There were no maps to guide them.

▲ The daring journeys made by explorers often led to slavery and death for the people they met. The lands the explorers claimed for their rulers were sometimes home to native peoples who had been living there for thousands of years.

## TRAVEL BUG

During the 18th and 19th centuries, explorers risked life and limb as they crossed stormy seas, treacherous jungles and barren deserts. Why? Many were scientific investigators, seeking out weird and wonderful plants and animals on the other side of the world. Others wanted to fill in blank areas on the map. Some were pilgrims who travelled to visit holy sites such as Mecca.

▶ Christian, Buddhist and Muslim missionaries were sent far and wide to convert people to their faith.

### SURVIVAL SKILLS

Many explorers relied on local guides and translators. When Vasco da Gama sailed from Africa to India in the fifteenth century, an Arab pilot helped him find his way.

# FIRST EXPLORERS

THE FIRST PEOPLE DID NOT FARM — THEY LIVED BY HUNTING ANIMALS AND GATHERING ROOTS AND BERRIES. HUNGER, THIRST AND CURIOSITY TURNED THEM INTO EXPLORERS.

It seems likely that around 100,000 years ago our ancestors left Africa and to find new places to live. Small family groups headed north across the Sahara Desert and then across south-east Asia. Over many thousands of years, they spread all over the world.

One reason why early humans were able to move across the globe is that during the Ice Age, 50,000 years ago, great sheets of ice near the Arctic trapped lots of water. That meant that sea levels were 90 m (30,000 ft) lower than they are today, revealing strips of land that formed bridges between the continents.

## LOOK CLOSER

Some experts believe Polynesian sailors, travelling in outrigger canoes, may have crossed the Pacific. This means they reached America about 1,000 years before Columbus.

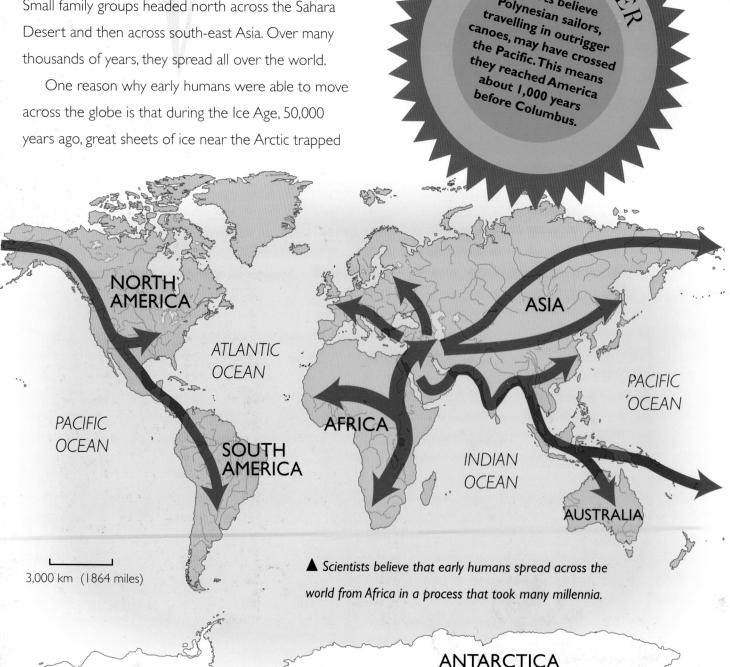

3,000 km (1864 miles)

▲ Scientists believe that early humans spread across the world from Africa in a process that took many millennia.

▲ Small groups of humans spread all over the world. They often followed the animals that they hunted for food.

## DREAMTIME

The Aboriginal peoples in Australia describe a time called 'Dreamtime'. This was when ancient spirits awoke and created the first plants, animals and humans. After the Ice Age, when the ice sheets melted and the seas returned, the Aboriginal peoples in Australia were cut off from the rest of the world.

◀ This bark painting shows three spirit figures from the Dreamtime legend.

# ANCIENT EXPLORERS

FIVE THOUSAND YEARS AGO, AROUND THE TIME THAT PEOPLE BEGAN TO WRITE THINGS DOWN, THEY BEGAN TO EXPLORE THE WORLD AROUND THEM.

The ancient Egyptians, sailing in large papyrus boats across the Mediterranean Sea and up and down the Nile River, traded gems, slaves and spices. Merchants from Phoenicia (now Lebanon and Syria) and Carthage sailed down the west coast of Africa. Later, the ancient Greeks sailed north to Britain and then to the Arctic Circle in search of metals, such as copper and tin.

In East Asia, from 100 BCE, merchants travelled across Central Asia on the Silk Road, while the Romans traded with both China and India for silk and spices. For the next thousand years, the seas were quiet – until the Vikings, eager to raid a new land, voyaged to America in the 10th century.

In 450 BCE, 30,000 settlers from Carthage colonized the west coast of Africa.

In 1470 BCE, Egyptian queen Hatshepsut sent traders to the Land of Punt.

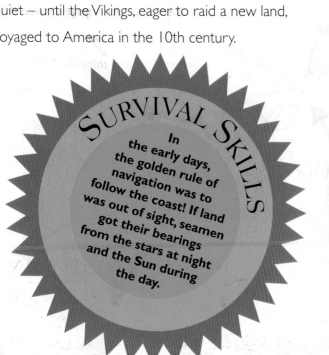

### SURVIVAL SKILLS

In the early days, the golden rule of navigation was to follow the coast! If land was out of sight, seamen got their bearings from the stars at night and the Sun during the day.

▲ From about 627 to 643, the Buddhist pilgrim Xuan Zang travelled 60,000 km (37,200 miles) across China and around India visiting sacred sites. He crossed the Takla Makan Desert, where he said that 'the rotting bones of dead men … point the way'.

▲ The Silk Road was an ancient caravan route, over 6,440 km (4,000 miles) long, that connected China, India, Central Asia and the Mediterranean Sea.

## THE ODYSSEY

Many ancient myths and legends may contain details about real people and places. Some historians believe that the voyages of the Greek hero Odysseus may be based on sailors' journeys around the Mediterranean Sea. It is also possible that the myth of Jason and the Argonauts may describe Greek voyages. The clashing rocks that almost crush their ship might refer to the narrow channel of the Bosphorus that separates Europe and Asia.

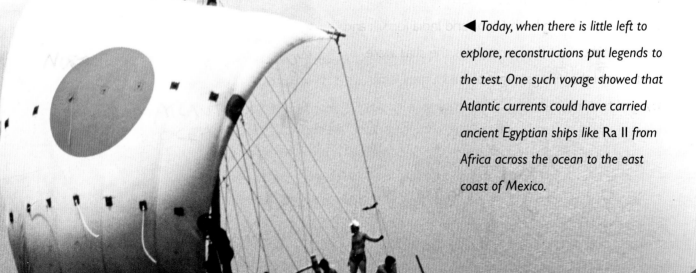

◄ Today, when there is little left to explore, reconstructions put legends to the test. One such voyage showed that Atlantic currents could have carried ancient Egyptian ships like Ra II from Africa across the ocean to the east coast of Mexico.

# AFRICA
### deserts • jungles • rivers

IN THE 19TH CENTURY, AFRICA WAS THE 'DARK CONTINENT'.

IT WAS DANGEROUS.

THE HEAT, DEADLY DISEASES AND WILD ANIMALS SCARED ALL BUT THE BRAVEST EXPLORERS.

# AFRICA OVERVIEW

EVEN IN THE EARLY 19TH CENTURY, MOST MAPS SHOWED AFRICA AS A BIG BLANK SPACE. BUT ARAB TRADERS HAD BEEN CROSSING THE SAHARA DESERT FOR HUNDREDS OF YEARS IN SEARCH OF RICHES.

In the late 18th century, a few European explorers began to cross the Sahara Desert. By the 19th century, modern medicines and guns encouraged explorers such as Mungo Park, John Speke and Henry Stanley to be even more adventurous. They followed great rivers inland and explored deep into the African jungle.

## SURVIVAL SKILLS

Some explorers dressed like the Arab traders of the Sahara. Others wore special clothes – pith helmets, tough safari jackets and boots – to keep leeches out.

## WHY GO THERE?

- **MONEY:** *Traders went to Africa in search of gold, spices and slaves.*

- **CURIOSITY:** *Early explorers wanted to solve puzzles such as the source of the River Nile.*

- **WILDLIFE:** *Some explorers wanted to record African plants and animals.*

- **EMPIRE:** *Many of the late 19th-century explorers led the way for European armies to conquer parts of Africa.*

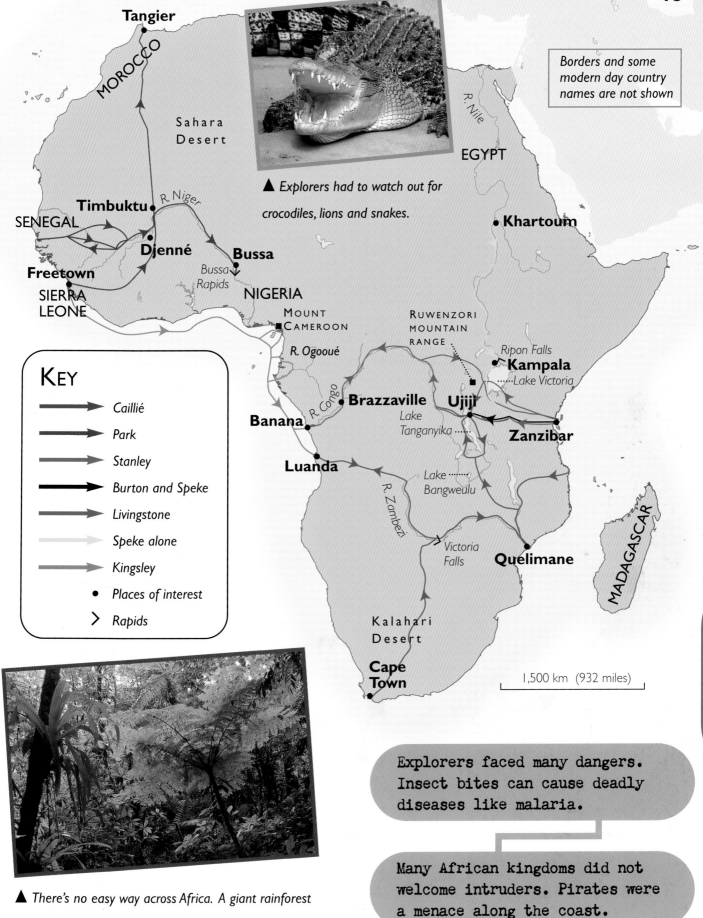

Tangier

MOROCCO

Sahara Desert

▲ Explorers had to watch out for crocodiles, lions and snakes.

Borders and some modern day country names are not shown

EGYPT

R. Nile

SENEGAL

Timbuktu

R. Niger

Khartoum

Djenné

Bussa
Bussa Rapids

Freetown

SIERRA LEONE

NIGERIA

MOUNT CAMEROON

R. Ogooué

RUWENZORI MOUNTAIN RANGE

Ripon Falls

Kampala
Lake Victoria

KEY

Caillié

Park

Stanley

Burton and Speke

Livingstone

Speke alone

Kingsley

• Places of interest

〉 Rapids

R. Congo

Brazzaville

Ujiji

Lake Tanganyika

Banana

Zanzibar

Luanda

Lake Bangweulu

R. Zambezi

Victoria Falls

Quelimane

MADAGASCAR

Kalahari Desert

Cape Town

1,500 km (932 miles)

▲ There's no easy way across Africa. A giant rainforest stretches across the centre. North and south are deserts.

Explorers faced many dangers. Insect bites can cause deadly diseases like malaria.

Many African kingdoms did not welcome intruders. Pirates were a menace along the coast.

# MUNGO PARK

**B**ORN IN THE SCOTTISH HILLS, MUNGO PARK COULD NEVER HAVE IMAGINED THAT HE WOULD ONE DAY FIND AND FOLLOW THE NIGER RIVER.

When in 1795 Park crossed the Sahara to embark on his adventure, he was held captive by a Moorish chief for four months, until he escaped. On 1 July, 1796, he finally reached the Niger. However, after tracing its course for 483 km (300 miles), half-starved and riddled by disease, Park was forced to turn back.

In 1805, Park set off again. Despite travelling 1,609 km (1,000 miles), the second expedition was a disaster. Only eight of its forty members survived to even reach the Niger. When tribesmen attacked their boats at the Bussa rapids, Park drowned.

## THE BIG KILL

**W**est Africa was known as the 'white man's grave' because thousands of Europeans who visited were struck down by malaria, yellow fever and dysentery. In 1821, 53 out of 79 missionaries sent to Sierra Leone, died. Their carpenter said, 'There is nothing but making coffins going on.'

## SURVIVAL SKILLS

Park was lucky to survive his first trip to Africa. He caught malaria. Doctors in Europe did not know how to treat the disease. A local trader nursed him through the illness.

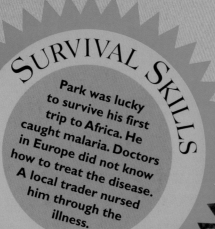

▶ Until Park visited the Niger, many European explorers thought that the river flowed west and joined the Senegal River. Local people knew the Niger's true course took it east.

▲ Park arrived in Africa still wearing traditional European dress. He used his top hat to keep his notes in!

Name: Mungo Park
Born: 10 September, 1771, Foulshiels, Selkirk, Scotland
Died: January 1806, near Bussa on the Niger River, Africa
Notable achievements:
Although trained as a surgeon, Park became an explorer after a chance meeting with the botanist Sir Joseph Banks. He was chosen by the African Association in London to find the course of the Niger. No-one in Europe knew whether the river flowed east or west. Park was also to visit the legendary city of Timbuktu. He never made it to Timbuktu, but he did follow the Niger River for 1,300 km (808 miles) and was the first European to discover that it flowed east. Between expeditions, Park published his book, *Travels in the Interior Districts of Africa* (1799), which became a bestseller and made him famous. The Duchess of Devonshire even wrote a poem in his honour!

On a previous expedition to the Niger, Daniel Houghton vanished without trace.

Park said, 'I shall discover the termination of the Niger or perish in the attempt.'

# RÉNÉ-AUGUSTE CAILLIÉ

SON OF A FRENCH BAKER, CAILLIÉ WAS ORPHANED AT 11. BUT AFTER READING THE BOOK *ROBINSON CRUSOE*, HE SET HIS HEART ON BEING AN EXPLORER.

When Caillié heard that a reward was being offered to the first man to reach Timbuktu, he decided to visit the legendary city himself. In 1827, after learning Arabic and disguising himself as a Muslim, he set off. Caillié joined a caravan and travelled over the Kong highlands to the city of Djenné, where he was delayed by illness for five months. Caillié finally reached Timbuktu on 20 April, 1838.

▶ *Caillié's disguise kept him out of trouble. However, he could only write his journal while pretending to read the Koran.*

Name: Réné-Auguste Caillié
Born: 19 November, 1799, Mauzé, western France
Died: 17 May, 1838, La Badère, France
Notable achievements: By the age of 20, Caillié had already travelled to West Africa twice. He became the first European to reach Timbuktu and come home alive. His achievement won a prize of 10,000 francs from the Geographical Society of Paris. Returning to France in 1828, Caillié became the mayor of his home town of Mauzé and wrote about his adventures in a book, *Travels through Central Africa to Timbuktu* (1830). Aged only 38, he died from a mystery illness he picked up in Africa.

▶ *Caillié hoped to see golden palaces at Timbuktu — but he found buildings made of mud. He stayed two weeks before heading home.*

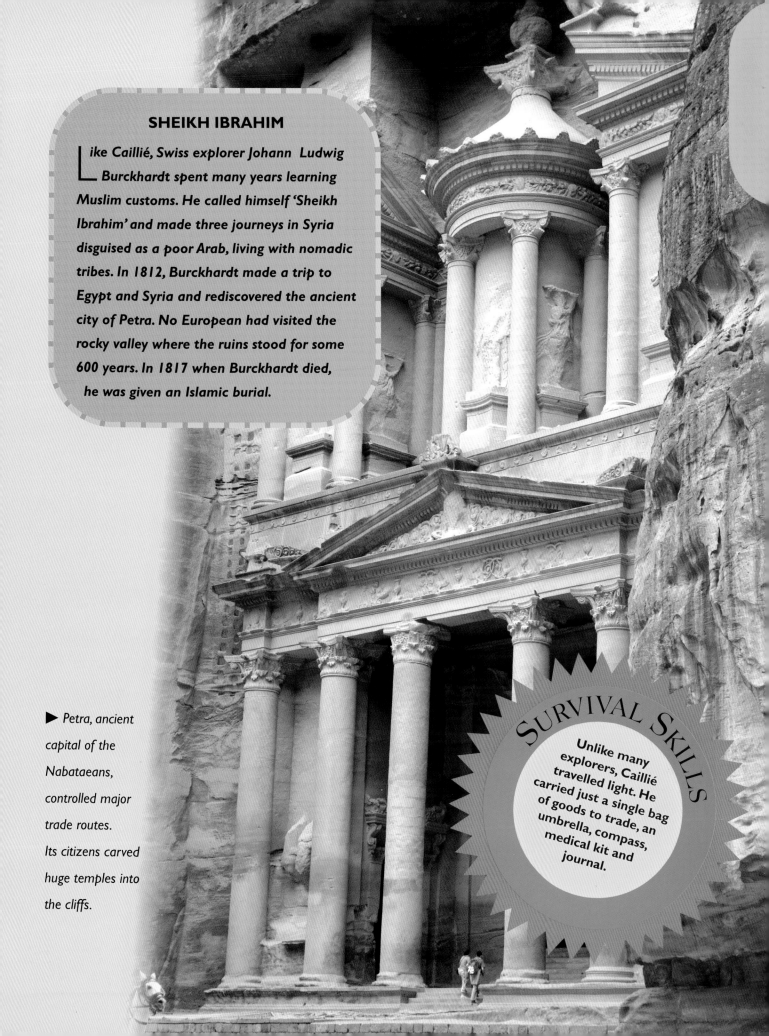

### SHEIKH IBRAHIM

Like Caillié, Swiss explorer Johann Ludwig Burckhardt spent many years learning Muslim customs. He called himself 'Sheikh Ibrahim' and made three journeys in Syria disguised as a poor Arab, living with nomadic tribes. In 1812, Burckhardt made a trip to Egypt and Syria and rediscovered the ancient city of Petra. No European had visited the rocky valley where the ruins stood for some 600 years. In 1817 when Burckhardt died, he was given an Islamic burial.

▶ Petra, ancient capital of the Nabataeans, controlled major trade routes. Its citizens carved huge temples into the cliffs.

## SURVIVAL SKILLS

Unlike many explorers, Caillié travelled light. He carried just a single bag of goods to trade, an umbrella, compass, medical kit and journal.

# BURTON AND SPEKE

THE NILE – THE WORLD'S LONGEST RIVER – FLOWS FOR **6,695** KM (**4,160** MILES). FOR MUCH OF ITS LENGTH, IT FLOWS THROUGH DESERT. SO WHERE DOES ALL THE WATER COME FROM?

Richard Burton and John Speke set out from Zanzibar in June 1857 to find out. Crossing deserts, marshes and mountains was tough, but after five months and almost 1,000 km (621 miles), the men finally reached Lake Tanganyika. Burton was crippled by malaria, so Speke explored the lake alone.

During their return journey, the two explorers heard of an even bigger lake. Burton was too ill to travel, however. Again, Speke pushed on alone. On 3 August, 1858, he came across a second lake, which he named Lake Victoria after his queen. Speke had found the source of the Nile – but he could not prove it.

## SURVIVAL SKILLS

An expedition needs lots of money. When Burton and Speke set off, they hired 200 local porters – but when their funds ran out, so did many of their men.

▼ *The 1990 film* Mountains of the Moon *depicts Burton (Patrick Bergin, left) and Speke's (Iain Glen, right) travels in Central Africa and the bitter rivalry between the two men.*

## FIGHT FOR LIFE

While Burton was recovering, Speke raced back to England to announce the source of the Nile. Burton was hopping mad. In 1862, Speke set off on another expedition to Lake Victoria. He found Ripon Falls, where the lake empties into the Nile, and confirmed his theory. Burton was still not convinced. He challenged Speke to a public debate, but the day before the event, Speke died in an accident. In a way, both men were right. Speke had found the source, but it was not the only one!

For most of the expedition Burton was ill and carried on a litter by porters.

Speke became deaf in one ear when removing a beetle caused an infection.

When Stanley explored Lake Victoria 12 years later, he confirmed it fed the Nile.

Name: Richard Francis Burton (above left)
Born: 19 March, 1821, Torquay, England
Died: 20 October, 1890, Trieste, Italy

Name: John Hanning Speke (above right)
Born: 3 May, 1821, Bideford, England
Died: 15 September, 1864, Bath, England

Notable achievements: The search for the source of the Nile made Burton and Speke famous. As well as Speke's discovery of Lake Victoria in 1858, the pair were the first Europeans to set eyes on Lake Tanganyika.

Speke returned to Africa in 1860. In 1862 he found the waters of Lake Victoria pouring down Ripon Falls into the Nile, but could not follow the river downstream due to a local war.

Burton spoke over 25 languages. He wrote over 50 books on a wide range of subjects, and translated the *Arabian Nights* stories into English.

▲ When Burton and Speke became the first Europeans to reach Lake Tanganyika, Speke was temporarily blinded by disease and couldn't see the water.

# LIVINGSTONE AND STANLEY

On 10 November, 1871, two of Africa's most famous explorers met at Ujiji on the shores of Lake Tanganyika. Henry Stanley stepped forward and said, 'Dr Livingstone, I presume.'

The missionary David Livingstone had been exploring Africa for four years when, in 1853, he set out from Cape Town. For six months, Livingstone crossed the Kalahari Desert and hacked his way through dense jungle. Battling sickness and hunger,

he arrived at Luanda on the west coast. Although offered a ship home, Livingstone would not leave his porters, who would have been made slaves. Instead he returned to the jungle, where he survived floods, crocodile attacks and spears thrown at him by locals.

## FINDING THE FALLS

Back in the jungle, Livingstone, helped by his friend Chief Sekeletu, drifted down the Zambezi River towards the east coast. On his way he came across an incredible set of waterfalls. The falls were so beautiful that Livingstone thought he had died and gone to heaven. He named Victoria Falls in honour of Queen Victoria.

◀ Livingstone was loved by many Africans who worked with him. In 1873, after he died, his heart was buried under a tree. His loyal servants Chuma and Susi carried his body over 1,600 km (994 miles) to the coast, where it was taken back to Britain by ship. He was buried in Westminster Abbey.

## SURVIVAL SKILLS

Livingstone found that boats were the quickest way to get around in the African interior. They may not have been the safest though – a hippo once tipped over his canoe!

◀ Local people call Victoria Falls the 'Smoke that Thunders'.

Name: David Livingstone

Born: 19 March, 1813, Blantyre, Scotland

Died: 1 May, 1873, near Lake Bangweulu, Zambia, Africa

Notable achievements: Livingstone went to Africa in 1841 to work as a missionary. His book, Missionary Travels and Researches in South Africa (1857), told of the horrors of the East African slave trade. He was one of the first Westerners to cross Africa from coast to coast and, after he visited Victoria Falls, the Royal Geographical Society awarded him a Gold Medal. From 1858 to 1869, he explored the Zambezi River and the region of Lake Tanganyika.

Henry Stanley was a Welsh-born American journalist. In 1871 his newspaper, the *New York Herald*, sent him to find Livingstone, who had not been heard of for some time. It took Stanley eight months to track the other man down. For a while the two men did some exploring together. Stanley was hooked. In 1874, a year after Livingstone's death, he set off with three officers and 350 porters and guides to explore the lakes of Central Africa. It took 100 days to reach Lake Victoria. After sailing around it, Stanley set off down the Congo River, travelling 11,265 km (7,000 miles) to the Atlantic coast. Despite bone-crunching rapids and running battles with local tribes, Stanley kept going. It was an incredible achievement.

## RACE FOR AFRICA

From 1879 to 1883, Stanley tricked many local chiefs along the Congo into handing their lands over to the Belgian king, Leopold II. Another explorer, Frenchman Pierre Savorgnan de Brazza (1852-1905), heard what was happening and warned his government. By 1885, using guns and offering money as bribes, Brazza had accumulated half a million square kilometres of land for the French. He also founded the city of Brazzaville. This claiming of land in Africa by European states is known as the 'Scramble for Africa'.

▼ *Stanley became famous by finding Dr Livingstone in 1871. He wrote in his journal that he greeted him with the words, 'Dr Livingstone, I presume?'*

## LOOK CLOSER

Explorers in Africa, such as Stanley and Livingstone, relied on a large number of guides and porters. A team leader called the 'kirangazi' organized the workers.

Name: Henry Morton Stanley

Born: 28 January, 1841, Denbigh, Wales

Died: 10 May, 1904, London, England

Notable achievement: Stanley solved one of the last great mysteries of African exploration in 1874 when he traced the course of the Congo River to the sea. His many books and articles made him a celebrity (though they were full of fibs about his achievements). However, unlike Livingstone, whom he found in 1871, Stanley often treated Africans badly. He tricked chiefs out of their lands to form the Congo Free State. The Belgian colony became infamous for its brutal treatment of Africans. When Stanley oversaw the building of a road in the Congo, he was such a harsh master that his men gave him a nickname - 'Breaker of Rocks'.

▶ King Leopold II made the Congo territory his own private property. He exploited its African inhabitants by forcing them to extract rubber from trees, from which he then made a fortune, selling it overseas.

# MARY KINGSLEY

Until she was 30, Mary Kingsley spent most of her life in London, caring for her mother. Soon after her parents died in 1892, however, she was on a cargo ship bound for West Africa.

Kingsley had used her father's library to learn about nature and local customs and persuaded the British Museum to pay for an expedition to study African wildlife. In 1893, she landed on what is now the coast of Nigeria and headed inland. Travelling deep into the rain forest, she searched for insects and fish. On a second trip, Kingsley went farther south and journeyed up the River Ogooué by steamboat and then canoe.

## NATURAL TALENT

Kingsley was not the first woman explorer to be mad about creepy crawlies and other unusual beasts. Maria Sibylla Merian (1699–1701) was already a famous wildlife painter in Holland when, at the age of 52, she set off with her daughter to South America. A team of slaves hacked a path for the two women through the thick rain forest. Merian's beautiful paintings showed many animals, such as the giant bird-eating spider, for the first time.

▼ Although Kingsley was the first European to climb Mount Cameroon, she was not interested in putting her name on a map by finding new rivers or mountain ranges.

Name: Mary Henrietta Kingsley
Born: 13 October, 1862, London, England
Died: 3 June, 1900, Simonstown, South Africa
Notable achievements: Kingsley made two trips to West and Central Africa at a time when the region was known as the 'white man's grave'. Driven by her interest in the local wildlife and peoples, she was the first outsider to meet the Fang tribe and the first woman to climb Mount Cameroon. In 1897, Kingsley wrote *Travels in West Africa*, which became an instant bestseller. The following year, she went to care for prisoners of war in South Africa. However, she caught a fever there and died.

▲ *Rather than march along in a big party like Henry Stanley, Kingsley slipped quietly into the areas she visited. This allowed her to reach places no European had been to before.*

## SURVIVAL SKILLS

Kingsley travelled in a tight-waisted dress. When she fell into a spiked animal trap, she said, 'It is at these moments that you realize the blessings of a good thick skirt!'

# ASIA
## mountains • plains • tundra

LARGE AREAS OF

CENTRAL ASIA WERE

UNKNOWN TO

OUTSIDERS UNTIL

THE 17TH CENTURY.

IT TOOK A WILL OF

IRON TO FACE THE

SEARING GOBI

DESERT AND

FIERCE NOMADS.

# ASIA OVERVIEW

FOR THOUSANDS OF YEARS, THE WEALTH OF CHINA AND INDIA ATTRACTED TRAVELLERS ACROSS ASIA.

In the Middle Ages, Muslim merchants followed the Silk Road. This ancient network of trails through mountains and deserts once joined the Roman Empire with China. It was later used by travellers such as Marco Polo. Other Europeans followed Arab sea routes across the Indian Ocean to South and East Asia.

To the north, the wastelands of Siberia were unknown until the 17th century, when Cossack pioneers pushed the borders of Russia farther and farther east.

## LOOK CLOSER

The capital of Tibet, Lhasa, was known as 'the Forbidden City': its religious leaders banned all foreigners from entering. The first Europeans to reach Lhasa had to go in disguise.

### WHY GO THERE?

- **RELIGION:** *Buddhist pilgrims such as Fa Xian travelled long distances to visit holy sites in China, Tibet, Nepal and India.*
- **TRADE:** *The Venetian Marco Polo went east in search of silk and spices.*
- **CURIOSITY:** *Ibn Battuta trekked around Asia just to see it for himself!*
- **EMPIRE:** *Vasco da Gama's voyages created a Portuguese empire in India and east Africa.*

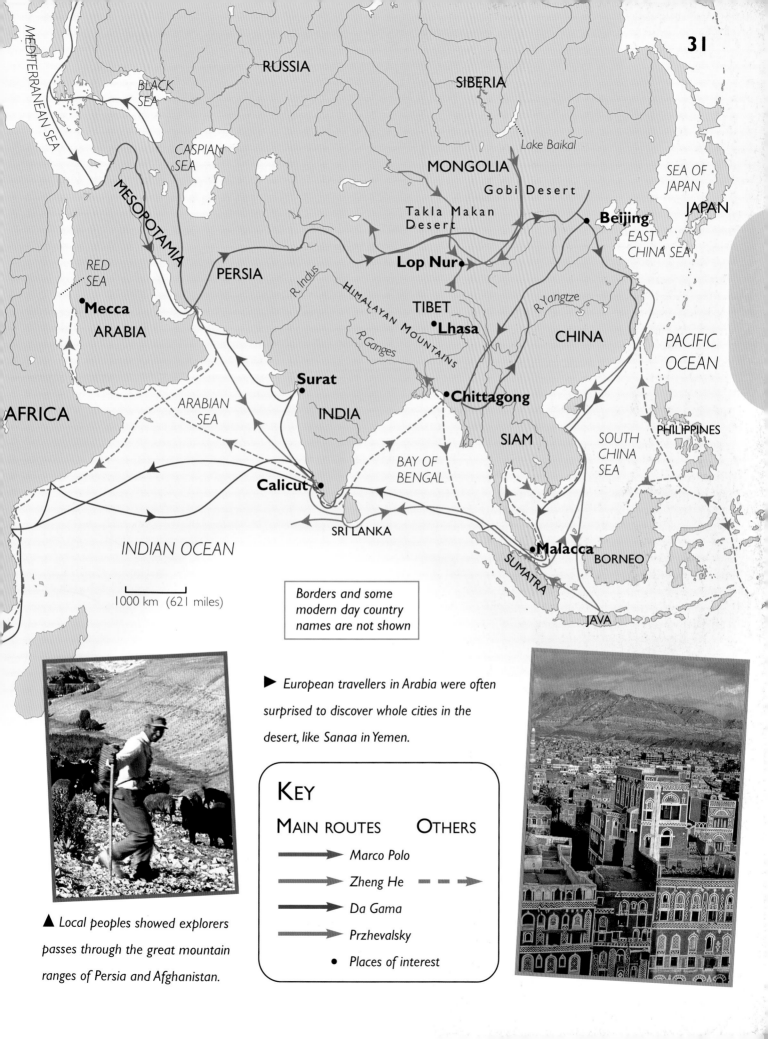

MEDITERRANEAN SEA

RUSSIA

SIBERIA

BLACK SEA

CASPIAN SEA

MONGOLIA

Lake Baikal

Gobi Desert

SEA OF JAPAN

JAPAN

MESOPOTAMIA

Takla Makan Desert

**Beijing**

EAST CHINA SEA

RED SEA

PERSIA

R. Indus

Lop Nur

R. Yangtze

**•Mecca**
ARABIA

HIMALAYAN MOUNTAINS

TIBET

**•Lhasa**

CHINA

PACIFIC OCEAN

R. Ganges

AFRICA

ARABIAN SEA

**Surat**

INDIA

**•Chittagong**

SIAM

SOUTH CHINA SEA

PHILIPPINES

BAY OF BENGAL

**Calicut**

INDIAN OCEAN

SRI LANKA

**•Malacca**

BORNEO

SUMATRA

JAVA

1000 km (621 miles)

Borders and some modern day country names are not shown

► European travellers in Arabia were often surprised to discover whole cities in the desert, like Sanaa in Yemen.

▲ Local peoples showed explorers passes through the great mountain ranges of Persia and Afghanistan.

KEY

MAIN ROUTES     OTHERS

→ *Marco Polo*

→ *Zheng He*     ⇢ - - ⇢

→ *Da Gama*

→ *Przhevalsky*

• Places of interest

# MARCO POLO

IN 1266, TWO ITALIAN MERCHANTS, NICCOLÒ AND MAFFEO POLO, TRAVELLED TO CHINA. THEY SO IMPRESSED THE MONGOL LEADER KUBLAI KHAN THAT HE ASKED THEM TO RETURN TO ITALY ON A MISSION TO SEE THE POPE.

In 1271, the Polos set off again, but this time Niccolò took his 16-year-old son, Marco. They sailed to the east coast of the Mediterranean and then trekked overland to Hormuz on the Persian Gulf. The Polos planned to sail to China, but were horrified by the leaky boats on offer. Instead, they plodded on through Persia (Iran) and Afghanistan. They crossed the Pamir Mountains and skirted the Takla Makan Desert. After four years, they reached the court of Kublai Khan in 1275. They presented the emperor with a gift of holy oil they had carried from Jerusalem.

Name: Marco Polo

Born: 15 September, 1254, Venice, Italy

Died: 9 January, 1324, Venice Italy

Notable achievements: In 1271, teenager Marco Polo set off for China. One of the very first Europeans to visit the region, he spent many years working for the Mongol ruler, Kublai Khan. He gathered information for the Khan on trading trips around China, which took him to the borders of Burma and Tibet. Polo returned to Venice in 1295, having covered some 39,000 km (24,240 miles). Three years later, he fought in a war against Venice's rival city Genoa, and was captured. While in prison, Marco dictated his travel stories to another prisoner, Rustichello. These were later made into a book called *Il Milione* (c.1299), also known as *The Travels*.

## LOOK CLOSER

When Marco Polo crossed the mountains in Afghanistan, he suffered from altitude sickness – an illness caused by the lack of oxygen in high places.

◄ *The Polos presented Kublai Khan with a letter from the Pope in reply to the khan's request for teachers in Christianity and Western customs.*

▼ *The Polos crossed the Gobi Desert as part of a camel caravan. Although the landscape was harsh, the route through the desert was well established.*

## TRAVELLER'S TALES

Marco Polo warned of 'spirit voices' that called to travellers as they crossed the Gobi Desert. He said that the voices drew people off the path – a deadly danger! Marco also investigated a cloth that did not burn in fire. Europeans believed that it was woven from the wool of a lizard-like desert creature called a salamander. Marco discovered that the cloth was made from stone. Today we know it as asbestos.

Kublai Khan trusted the Polos and asked them to work for him. As they travelled around East Asia, Marco wrote down the local customs and sent reports to the emperor. Marco described a black rock that burned for hours (coal) and an amazing postal system: relay riders on horseback could carry messages 185 km (115 miles) in a single day.

Marco also marvelled at how Kublai Khan lived. His dining hall was covered in gold and silver and could hold 6,000 guests. After 17 years, the Polos got homesick. Kublai Khan asked them to carry out one last mission on their way home. They escorted a Mongol princess to marry a prince in Persia. Finally, the Polos returned to Venice in the winter of 1295.

▼ *When Kublai Khan went hunting, he took 10,000 riders and 5,000 dogs with him. In his private park, tigers were trained to chase deer.*

### STRANGE LAND

Marco Polo's tales are full of dragons, unicorns and strange men with tails! However, he also talks about real people and places. He says that Kublai Khan was a plump man with a face 'fair and ruddy like a rose'. Marco describes the explosive bang made by bamboos as they burn, the tattoos loved by the Burmese and a battle between Mongol horsemen and rebels who rode on elephants. On his deathbed, Marco said: 'I have not told the half of what I saw'.

The Khan had many wives. New wives were chosen by scouts from 400 to 500 women.

Polo admired Chinese paper money and their beautifully painted china bowls.

◀ The Great Wall was built to keep invaders out of China, but it did not stop the Mongol armies. Kublai Khan's kingdom was part of a Mongol empire that stretched across Asia to Europe.

▶ The Mongols fought on horseback and were fierce warriors. At Nishapur in Persia they made a huge pyramid out of the skulls of their victims.

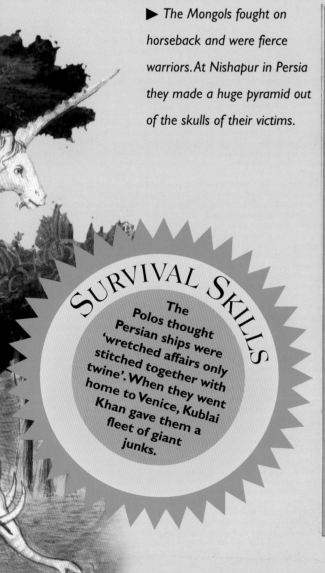

## SURVIVAL SKILLS

The Polos thought Persian ships were 'wretched affairs only stitched together with twine'. When they went home to Venice, Kublai Khan gave them a fleet of giant junks.

Combat à pied - Perse mongole début du XVᵉ siècle, Cott. 9, Ober

# IBN BATTUTA

IN 1325, 21-YEAR-OLD IBN BATTUTA SET OFF FROM MOROCCO TO VISIT MECCA. IN EGYPT, HE MET A MERCHANT WHO SUGGESTED A VISIT TO INDIA AND CHINA. 'WHY NOT?' THOUGHT IBN BATTUTA, AND OFF HE WENT.

After reaching Mecca and wandering 7,000 km (4,350 miles) around Mesopotamia (now Iraq), Ibn Battuta sailed down the east coast of Africa. He passed the port of Zeila, which he called 'the stinkiest town in the world'. He decided to visit India by travelling overland across Central Asia. He joined the great caravan of the Mongol Khan (ruler) Ozbeg, who was so rich that even his third wife had 5,000 guards and 400 wagons to carry her slaves and her clothes!

Name: Ibn Battuta
Born: Tangiers, Morocco, 1304
Died: Fez, Morocco, 1377
Notable achievement: Ibn Battuta was the most famous traveller of his age. He explored Egypt, East Africa, Syria, Arabia, Siberia, India and China. He saw more of the world than anyone before him, travelling an incredible 120,000 km (74,500 miles). His reason for going – 'it seemed like a good idea'! Battuta's first journey took 24 years. He returned home to Morocco but set off again two years later to explore west Africa. Home at last, he wrote a book called *Rihla* ('travels').

▼ Ibn Battuta's amazing journeys began with a hajj, or pilgrimage, to the Islamic holy city of Mecca.

# IBN BATTUTA

▲ Ibn Battuta's great journeys took him to the lands of every Muslim ruler in the world.

▼ He crossed the Red Sea in an Arab sailing boat called a dhow. Muslim sailors were famed for their skills.

## CHILLY CROSSING

Ibn Battuta spent the winter of 1332 in southern Russia with Khan Ozbeg's caravan. The weather was freezing. Every time he tried to wash his face, the water turned to ice! The next year, he crossed the Hindu Kush mountains to India. He had to lay a trail of cloths to stop his camels sinking into the snow.

## SURVIVAL SKILLS

Ibn Battuta survived the harsh winter in central Asia by wearing three fur coats, two pairs of trousers, two layers of socks and boots lined with bearskin!

In India, the powerful Sultan of Delhi liked Ibn Battuta so much he made him Chief Judge. However, Ibn Battuta soon spent all his salary. Fearing the Sultan's anger, he fled into the desert. He survived without food for 40 days! Luckily the Sultan forgave Ibn Battuta and asked him to visit China on his behalf.

Ibn Battuta reached China via the Maldive Islands, Sri Lanka and Sumatra. On the way he was shipwrecked, attacked by bandits and was nearly beheaded! He visited Guangzou in the south of China and may have got to Beijing. He described Chinese inventions such as porcelain and paper money.

Ibn Battuta returned to Egypt in 1347, as the Black Death was spreading across the Middle East. Without catching even a sniffle, Battuta arrived in Morocco in 1348.

## LOOK CLOSER

Ibn Battuta arrived in Delhi in late 1333. The Sultan celebrated by firing coins into the crowd from the catapults on the backs of his elephants. What a welcome!

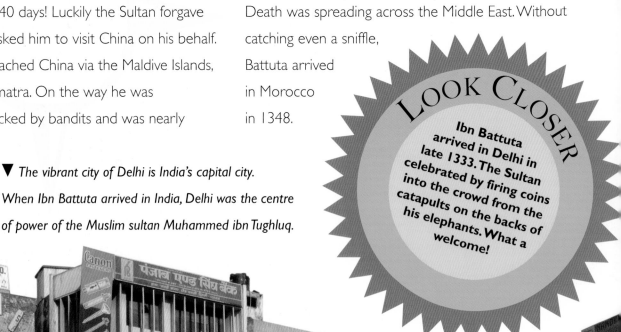

▼ The vibrant city of Delhi is India's capital city. When Ibn Battuta arrived in India, Delhi was the centre of power of the Muslim sultan Muhammed ibn Tughluq.

## ITCHY FEET!

Back home in Morocco Ibn Battuta could not sit still while there were still places to see. In 1351, he set off on a final trek, travelling 16,000 km (10,000 miles) across the Sahara Desert by camel to Mali and Timbuktoo. He sailed along the River Niger, spotting hippopotamuses and crocodiles along the way.

Ibn Battuta was a charmer! He married and divorced many times during his travels.

He arrived in India with a harem of wives but left them behind when he went to China!

## SINBAD THE SAILOR

Ibn Battuta's incredible journey is matched by the legends of Sinbad, a sailor from Basra (now in Iraq). These stories were based on the experiences of Muslim sailors in the Indian Ocean. Sinbad meets all sorts of horrors, including human-eating apes, enormous dive-bombing birds called rocs and an island that turns out to be a huge fish!

▶ Sinbad's adventures have been filmed many times. Douglas Fairbanks Jr. played him in 1947.

# ZHENG HE

IN 1405, THE CHINESE ADMIRAL ZHENG HE LED A FLEET OF 62 GIANT JUNKS, 225 SMALLER VESSELS AND 28,000 MEN TO INDIA AND EAST AFRICA.

His ships carried scientists, doctors and merchants, as well as sailors and soldiers. Zheng He's army was enough to frighten any enemy, but he was a clever diplomat. He handed out gifts of Chinese silk and porcelain, and made offerings to local gods.

Along the way, Zheng He captured a feared pirate and visited the Islamic holy city of Mecca. When he returned home, his ships were laden with ivory, pearls, precious stones, spices and medicines.

▲ The biggest treasure junks were almost 137 m (450 ft) long and 55 m (180 ft) wide – that's 10 times the size of Columbus's Santa Maria.

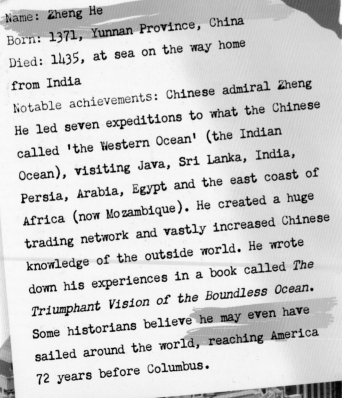

Name: Zheng He

Born: 1371, Yunnan Province, China

Died: 1435, at sea on the way home from India

Notable achievements: Chinese admiral Zheng He led seven expeditions to what the Chinese called 'the Western Ocean' (the Indian Ocean), visiting Java, Sri Lanka, India, Persia, Arabia, Egypt and the east coast of Africa (now Mozambique). He created a huge trading network and vastly increased Chinese knowledge of the outside world. He wrote down his experiences in a book called *The Triumphant Vision of the Boundless Ocean.* Some historians believe he may even have sailed around the world, reaching America 72 years before Columbus.

## FAIR TRADE

Unlike many European explorers, Zheng He's main aim was to promote trade and make allies. However after the death of the emperor in 1424, foreign voyages were banned. Zheng He's great fleet rotted and some of his notes and charts were destroyed. The age of Chinese exploration was over, leaving the way clear for European adventurers.

▶ Zheng He brought back a giraffe from Africa as a gift for the Emperor from the kingdom of Malindi.

## SURVIVAL SKILLS

By 1000 CE, 300 years before sailors in Europe, most Chinese sailors were using compasses. In the 1300s they also had a clever system of maps based on a grid.

Zheng He reached East Africa almost 100 years before any Europeans.

He set up trade routes from Thailand to Sri Lanka along the East African coast.

◀ After Zheng He's death, international trade ceased in China and great natural harbours such as Hong Kong were neglected. Gradually the Chinese forgot how to build large sea-worthy vessels.

# VASCO DA GAMA

VASCO DA GAMA WAS A GREAT SAILOR, BUT A VIOLENT MAN. HE LEFT LISBON WITH FOUR SHIPS IN 1497 AND IN JUST FOUR MONTHS ROUNDED THE SOUTHERN TIP OF AFRICA INTO THE INDIAN OCEAN, FARTHER THAN ANY PREVIOUS EXPEDITIONS.

But when da Gama stopped to pick up supplies on the East African coast, he picked a fight with locals. Later, his ships fired on a crowd at Mozambique, and he attacked several Arab ships at Mombasa.

Blown by the monsoon wind, da Gama reached India in just 23 days. The ruler of Calicut laughed at the worthless presents da Gama offered him. Da Gama was ready for a fight, but in the end he headed home with a cargo of spices. Not content with this, he looted several ships along the Indian coast on his way home!

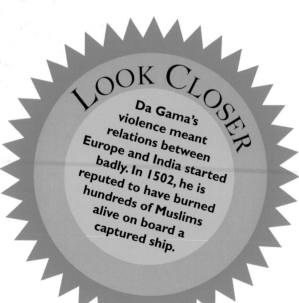

## LOOK CLOSER

Da Gama's violence meant relations between Europe and India started badly. In 1502, he is reputed to have burned hundreds of Muslims alive on board a captured ship.

Name: Vasco da Gama

Born: 1460, Sines, Portugal

Died: 24 December, 1524, Cochin, India

Notable achievements: Portuguese navigator Vasco da Gama was the first European to travel by sea from Portugal to India. This route allowed Europeans to trade with East Asia without having to make the long journey overland along the 'Silk Road'. Da Gama's voyage also meant that Portugal controlled the trade route to India for the next 250 years.

Da Gama was made 'Admiral of the Indian Ocean' and went back to India with 20 ships. There he destroyed a fleet of Arab ships and set up trading posts at Calicut and Goa. He sailed back to Portugal with a large haul of treasure and was made a count in 1519.

◀ *Modern weapons gave Europeans a big advantage. The iron cannonballs fired by da Gama's ships blasted holes in Arab and Indian vessels, which had no gunpowder weapons.*

## AN ACCIDENTAL DISCOVERY

Between da Gama's voyages, another Portuguese also sailed to India. Pedro Alvares Cabral (c.1467–c.1520) set sail in 1500. He headed into the Atlantic Ocean, where da Gama said the winds were more helpful than near the African coast. But Cabral went so far southwest that he discovered Brazil! He claimed the land for Portugal, before turning east to India, where he traded with merchants at the port of Cochin.

▼ *Examples of Portuguese-influenced architecture can still be seen at Goa today.*

Da Gama hired an Arab pilot to guide him across the Indian Ocean to Calicut.

During da Gama's voyage home to Lisbon, he lost two ships and 55 men.

# NIKOLAI PRZEWALSKI

NIKOLAI PRZEWALSKI, AN OFFICER IN THE RUSSIAN ARMY, WAS DETERMINED TO REACH LHASA, THE CAPITAL OF TIBET.

He liked to travel at speed. In one expedition, he covered 24,000 km (14,916 miles) in just three years. Deserts and mountains made the going tough and food was always scarce. It got so bad that his camels tore open their own saddles to eat the stuffing!

Przewalski zig-zagged his way across Central Asia, mapping it for the Russian government. He became the first outsider to explore the great salt lake of Lop Nor and to visit the 'Caves of the Thousand Buddhas' in Dunhuang. Although he never did make it to Lhasa, Przewalski charted a huge chunk of Central Asia that until then was just a blank area on a map.

▲ During his travels, Przewalski took scientific notes and collected plants. He discovered wild herds of Bactrian camels as well as the Przewalski's horse named after him.

## LOOK CLOSER

Przewalski was a trigger-happy hunter. He shot yaks, wolves, deer – and anything else that moved. He celebrated New Year's Day in 1885 by shooting 23 orongo antelope.

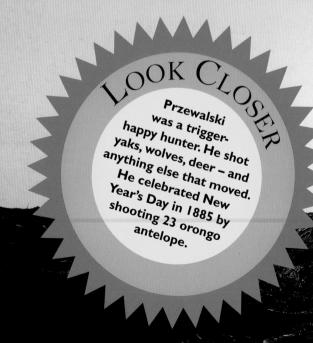

Name: Nikolai Mikhaylovich Przewalski
Born: 31 March, 1839, Smolensk, Russia
Died: 20 October, 1888, Karakol, Kyrgyzstan
Notable achievements: Between 1871 and 1888, Przewalski made five great treks across Central Asia and became the first outsider to explore this vast wilderness of deserts, mountains and frozen rivers. In his first expedition he travelled south, crossing the Gobi Desert before exploring the great Chinese rivers, the Hwang He (Yellow River) and the Yangtze. Przewalski then went over the Tian Shan mountains and, skirting around the Takla Makan Desert, became the first European to visit the salt lake of Lop Nor since Marco Polo.

## THIRSTY WORK

Like Przewalski, Swedish explorer Sven Hedin (1890-1935) was a map-maker. Hedin explored large areas of Tibet, the Himalayas and the ancient Silk Road. He found the ancient Chinese city of Loulan in the Takla Makan Desert. During the trip, he and a colleague ran out of water. Desperately thirsty, Hedin was forced to crawl across the sand on all fours. When he finally found an oasis, he filled his boots with water and carried them back to his companion.

▶ Hedin seems to have been the first person to realize that the Himalayas are a single mountain range.

▼ During his first expedition, when Przewalski explored the great salt lake of Lop Nur, he took three Cossacks with him. These skilled horsemen could cope with the tough terrain of the region.

Just 260 km (162 miles) from Lhasa, officials turned Przewalski away.

Lhasa was sacred to Tibet's Buddhists, who barred all Europeans until 1904.

Przewalski's maps helped the Russian Army to plot against the Chinese.

# ISABELLA BIRD

I N THE 19TH CENTURY, WOMEN WERE CONSIDERED TOO WEAK TO MAKE DANGEROUS JOURNEYS. ISABELLA BIRD WAS ONE OF SEVERAL FEMALE EXPLORERS WHO PROVED THE THEORY WRONG.

Bird was a sickly child and it was on the advice of her doctor that she first set off on her travels at the age of 23. Bird visited Hawaii, Australia and North America, riding 1,300 km (808 miles) across the Rocky Mountains. However, Bird's greatest adventure began in 1890, at the age of 58. She joined an army officer in a winter trek from Baghdad to Tehran (now the capitals of Iraq and Iran). It was a terrible journey. Despite the protection of a cork hat, snow spectacles and a woollen face mask, she was frozen day and night. When her mule finally tottered into Tehran, Bird was so stiff she could hardly get off!

Name: Isabella Lucy Bird
Born: 15 October, 1831, Boroughbridge, England
Died: 7 October, 1904, Edinburgh, Scotland
Notable achievements: Although Bird did not discover any unknown places, she had the most amazing adventures at a time when women were expected to stay at home. She visited Japan, China, Vietnam, Korea, India, Tibet, Turkey, Morocco, Australia and Hawaii, as well as making long journeys across North America. Bird paid for her travels by writing about them. Often featured in magazines, she became a household name and was the first woman asked to join the Royal Geographical Society, in 1892.

Bird headed up her own caravan through northern Iran, Kurdistan and Turkey.

In the Rockies, Bird became good friends with a one-eyed outlaw called Jim Nugent.

▼ After reaching Tehran, Bird spent another six months making her way back to Istanbul in Turkey.

▼ Bird visited Tehran, in the shadow of the Elburz
Mountains, after the long trek from Baghdad. She
_____ man, rather
_____ she visited
_____ a ladder to
_____ her.

**___DE BELL**

_) was a real-life Indiana
_s exploring ancient ruins in
_ia (now Iraq). In 1913, Bell
_ert, surviving fights with
_sh officials. She became the
_ert Arabs, who called her
'the Daughter of the Desert'. Bell could even enter areas
forbidden to men, such as harems. In World War I, she
became an advisor to the British Army, which wanted to
make alliances with the Arabs.

▶ After World War I, Gertrude Bell helped the British create modern Iraq.

# OCEANIA
outback • islands • oceans

AUSTRALIA WAS A LONG, TERRIFYING SEA VOYAGE FROM EUROPE. BUT ONCE EUROPEANS REACHED THE CONTINENT, EXPLORERS SOON BRAVED ITS DESERTS AND SWAMPS.

# OCEANIA OVERVIEW

FROM 400 CE, POLYNESIANS SAILED ACROSS THE PACIFIC OCEAN, MAKING SHORT HOPS FROM ISLAND TO ISLAND. THREE HUNDRED YEARS LATER, FERDINAND MAGELLAN OPENED THE OCEAN TO EUROPEANS.

Some early European explorers reached Australia, but James Cook was the first to realise he had found a new continent, in 1770. Settlers soon arrived, but the rainforests of the north and the deserts of the centre were a graveyard for explorers until well into the 19th century.

## SURVIVAL SKILLS

If heat and thirst didn't kill an explorer crossing the Australian desert, snakes and scorpions might. In the north lay crocodile-infested swamps, malaria and thick forests.

## WHY GO THERE?

- **LAND:** *Early Pacific voyagers sailed from island to island in search of a new home.*

- **TRADE:** *Merchants wanted to find quick routes to East Asia – just as Columbus had hoped to do!*

- **SCIENCE:** *James Cook set out to track the movement of the planet Venus, record local wildlife and find the 'Great Southern Continent'.*

- **CONQUEST:** *By the 19th century, explorers were more interested in empire than science or trade.*

◀ *Thick mangroves in northern Australia prevented explorers from the interior reaching the coast.*

**KEY**

**MAIN ROUTES**

⟶ Cook

⟶ Flinders

⟶ Burke & Wills

⟶ Leichhardt

● Places of interest

▲ *The Great Barrier Reef is a tourist attraction today – but for early explorers it was a hazard where many ships were wrecked.*

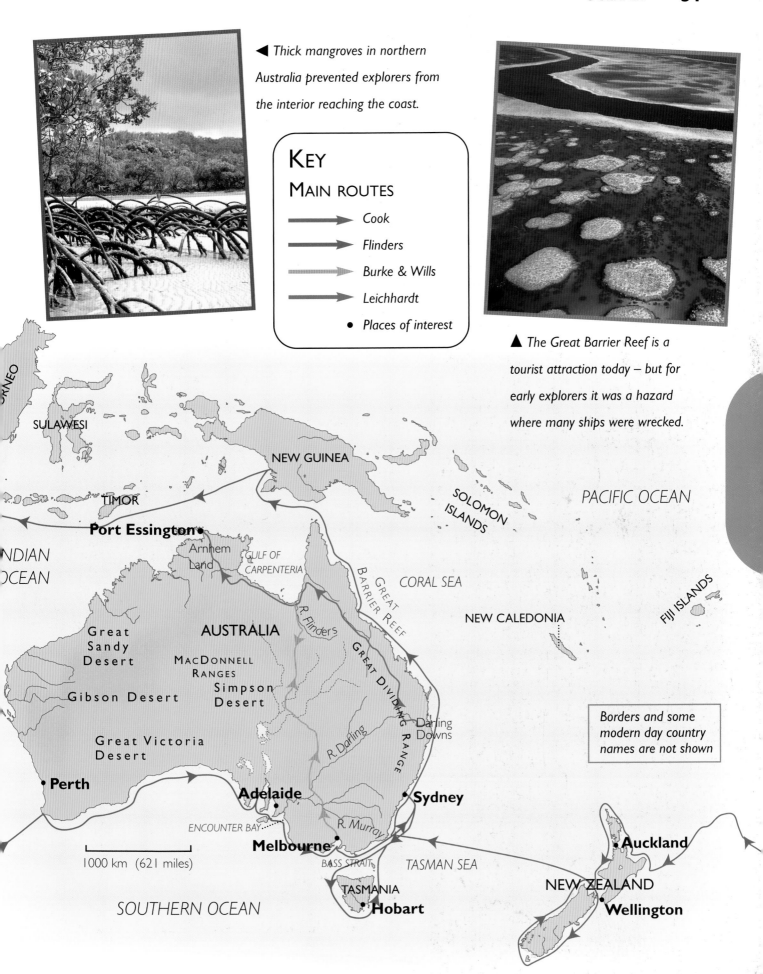

BORNEO

SULAWESI

NEW GUINEA

TIMOR

SOLOMON ISLANDS

PACIFIC OCEAN

**Port Essington** ●

Arnhem Land

GULF OF CARPENTERIA

CORAL SEA

INDIAN OCEAN

GREAT BARRIER REEF

NEW CALEDONIA

FIJI ISLANDS

R. Flinders

**AUSTRALIA**

Great Sandy Desert

MACDONNELL RANGES

Simpson Desert

GREAT DIVIDING RANGE

Gibson Desert

Darling Downs

Great Victoria Desert

R. Darling

*Borders and some modern day country names are not shown*

● **Perth**

**Adelaide** ●

**Sydney**

ENCOUNTER BAY

R. Murray

● **Auckland**

1000 km (621 miles)

**Melbourne** ●

BASS STRAIT

*TASMAN SEA*

**NEW ZEALAND**

TASMANIA

SOUTHERN OCEAN

**Hobart**

● **Wellington**

# JAMES COOK

O N 26 AUGUST, 1768, JAMES COOK SET OFF IN THE SHIP *ENDEAVOUR*. HIS MISSION WAS TO RECORD THE PLANET VENUS AS IT PASSED IN FRONT OF THE SUN. THE BEST PLACE TO OBSERVE THE RARE EVENT WAS TAHITI, AN ISLAND IN THE SOUTH PACIFIC.

Eight months later, Cook reached his destination. There he tracked Venus before opening a packet of secret orders. They told him to search for the 'Great Southern Continent'.

The *Endeavour* pushed south until the icy weather froze its crew's hands to the rigging. Cook turned east. On 6 October, 1769, Cook spotted the islands we call New Zealand. Cook spent six months mapping the coast then headed home. Three weeks later, he saw land again. Cook had discovered Australia!

▲ Cook tried hard to win the trust of the local peoples. He had a life-long friendship with the Maoris of New Zealand.

▼ During his second voyage to the Pacific, Cook marvelled at the giant statues, or moai, found on Easter Island.

## DANGEROUS DAYS

A s Cook sailed north along the east coast of Australia, the Endeavour ran aground on coral in the Great Barrier Reef. Although it floated off, the ship was leaking badly. Clever Cook tied a sail around the bottom of the ship. His crew got the ship into shallow water, where they could repair it. Soon after, Cook sailed back through the reef towards modern Indonesia. When they got there, the whole crew was struck down by malaria and dysentery!

▶ Cook took with him a team of scientists that included the botanist Joseph Banks. When the Endeavour first dropped anchor off Australia, the number of new plant species Banks found on the shore gave the coastline its name – Botany Bay.

## LOOK CLOSER

The Gogo-Yimidir Aborigines who were living on the west coast of Australia told Cook about a 'jumping wild dog'. Cook's crew named the animal a kangaroo.

Name: James Cook

Born: 27 October, 1728, Marston, England

Died: 14 February, 1779, Hawaii

Notable achievements: In three amazing journeys, Cook discovered more about the Earth's surface than any other explorer. In his first voyage (1768-71), he found Australia and charted the coastline of New Zealand – all 3,860 km (2,399 miles) of it. His charts were so accurate they were still in use 120 years later. On his second voyage (1772-75), Cook explored the Pacific, visiting Easter Island, and sailed all the way around Antarctica, although he never saw it. On his third voyage (1776-79), Cook went in search of the Northwest Passage around Canada and Alaska. This voyage ended in disaster when Cook was killed by Hawaiians after a quarrel over a stolen boat.

# MATTHEW FLINDERS

AFTER READING DANIEL DEFOE'S BOOK *ROBINSON CRUSOE*, MATTHEW FLINDERS DREAMED OF BECOMING A SAILOR. HE JOINED THE BRITISH NAVY IN 1789, AGED JUST 15.

Flinders met George Bass, a ship's surgeon, on the voyage to Australia. In 1796, the two men explored the coast south of Sydney in a boat called the *Tom Thumb*. The tiny craft was only 2.5 m (8 ft) long! Two years later they sailed all the way around Tasmania.

Flinders was asked to chart the Australian coast in 1801, a voyage filled with danger. His crew were attacked, and eight men drowned looking for fresh water. Many others fell sick with dysentery. The journey home was no easier – Flinders's first ship was shipwrecked. Then, calling into Mauritius, he was put in prison as a spy for six years before finally reaching Britain in 1810

▼ The coast of Tasmania. Flinders proved it was an island by sailing round it.

## LOOK CLOSER

Flinders married his wife Ann just three months before he left for Australia. It was nine long years before he saw her again!

Name: Matthew Flinders
Born: Donnington,
Lincolnshire,
England, 1774
Died: London,
England, 1814
Notable achievement:

Matthew Flinders was the first person to sail around Australia. He suggested the name 'Australia' for the new continent, which was adopted in 1824. Flinders and George Bass were the first Europeans to sail all the way around Tasmania. In 1801, Flinders was asked to make a survey of the coastline of Australia. He completed this in 1803. His charts were so good, they were used for many years after his death.

Tasmania used to be called Van Diemen's Land, after an earlier Dutch explorer.

It took Flinders two years to sail all the way round Australia. Amazing!

## A LEAKING SHIP

In December 1801, Flinders set off in the Investigator from Cape Leeuwin on the southwest tip of Australia. After charting the south coast he headed up the eastern side. He was eager to continue, but his ship let him down. It was leaking all the time. By March 1803 Flinders had charted the northern coast as far as Arnhem Bay at the very top. His ship was leaking so badly, he had to give up detailed mapping of the coast.

# LUDWIG LEICHHARDT

IN 1848, PRUSSIAN EXPLORER LUDWIG LEICHHARDT LEFT A SHEEP STATION WHERE HE WAS STAYING AND VANISHED INTO THE AUSTRALIAN OUTBACK. OVER THE NEXT 90 YEARS, NINE SEARCH PARTIES TRIED TO LOCATE HIM. HIS BODY WAS NEVER FOUND.

Leichhardt was born in what is now Germany. In 1842 he travelled to Australia to study its rocks and wildlife and in 1844, he organized an expedition to explore northeast Australia. In December 1845, after a trek of 5,000 km (3,107 miles), he reached Port Essington in the Northern Territory.

▼ Early settlers hoped the centre of Australia would make good farmland, like the Great Plains that stretch across North America. However, most of Central Australia is a huge desert, known as the outback or the 'never-never'.

During his second expedition, which started in December 1846, Leichhardt planned to cross Australia from east to west. It took him seven months to travel just 800 km (497 miles), however. Drought, malaria and lack of food forced him to turn back.

When Leichhardt set off again, in March 1848, his party of six crossed Australia's Great Dividing Range. They stayed at a sheep station – but then vanished after they continued their trip. To this day, no one knows what happened to Leichhardt or his men.

Leichhardt carried little food - he was determined to live off the land.

In the outback, Leichhardt could hunt lizards, emus, kangaroos and flying foxes.

Unfortunately Leichhardt was a poor bushman who got lost easily!

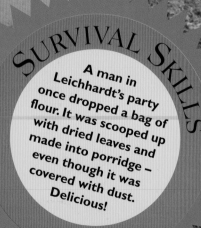

SURVIVAL SKILLS

A man in Leichhardt's party once dropped a bag of flour. It was scooped up with dried leaves and made into porridge – even though it was covered with dust. Delicious!

## WHAT KILLED LEICHHARDT?

It could have been lack of water or food, sudden floods or the desert heat that killed Leichhardt. No one will ever know. Search parties found horse bones, a tomahawk and even an 'L' carved onto trees, but no real proof of what had happened. Almost 50 years later, searchers in the Great Sandy Desert met Aborigines who showed them a tent peg, a tin matchbox and part of a saddle. Were they Leichhardt's? No one knows for sure.

Name: Friedrich Wilhelm Ludwig Leichhardt

Born: 23 October, 1813, Trebatch, Prussia

Died: probably 1848, Australian outback

Notable achievements: In his first expedition, Ludwig Leichhardt explored large parts of Australia's interior. This expedition led the way for a wave of farmers and other settlers into what is now Queensland and the Northern Territory. Leichhardt was the first European to cross northeastern Australia, but he failed in his attempt to cross Australia from east to west.

# BURKE AND WILLS

IN 1859, THE SOUTH AUSTRALIAN PARLIAMENT OFFERED A REWARD FOR A TEAM TO CROSS AUSTRALIA FROM SOUTH TO NORTH. AN EXPEDITION WAS SOON ORGANIZED, LED BY ROBERT BURKE.

By mid-November, Burke and William Wills had set up camp at Cooper's Creek, about halfway across Australia. Burke and Wills, with two others, decided to make a dash for the north coast, leaving a support team to wait three months for their return. After trekking for six weeks around the edge of the Stony Desert by camel, the four men reached the forests and swamps of the north. They came to a river and tasting salty water realized they must be near the sea – but without a boat there was no easy way forward. Instead, they had to turn back and return south.

Name: Robert O'Hara Burke (below left)
Born: 1821, St. Clerah's, Co. Galway, Ireland
Died: June, 1861, Australia

Name: William John Wills (below right)
Born: 1834, Totnes, Devon, England
Died: 1861, Australia

Notable achievement: Burke and Wills were the first explorers to make the South-North crossing of Australia. They did not actually reach the sea on the north coast, but carved a marker into a nearby tree. However, both men died lonely deaths from starvation and heat exhaustion. Burke had little experience as an explorer and did not know how to live off the land. Wills was more capable, leading the party to Cooper's Creek, but never questioning Burke's leadership.

## SURVIVAL SKILLS

To prevent scurvy, Burke and Wills took lots of lime juice with them on the trip. Scurvy is caused by a lack of Vitamin C. It rots your gums and makes your legs weak.

## RACE FOR HONOUR

Burke and Wills made a mistake when they impatiently embarked on their journey north. The weather was hot and dry, and it would have been safer to stay put until summer was over. But Burke was impatient. He had heard of a rival expedition, led by John McDouall Stuart, and was afraid that Stuart might reach the coast first. Burke was under pressure from his sponsors, who had told him, 'The honour of Victoria is in your hands'.

▲ Burke took six camels to northern Australia. When supplies ran out, the men ate the animals.

▼ No one knew what was in the centre of Australia. Some people thought there might be an inland sea. In fact, Burke and Wills found desert, although Aborigines pointed out the best waterholes and travelling was not difficult.

Expedition supplies included 80 pairs of shoes, 20 beds, 30 hats and 57 buckets.

There were also wagons that turned into rafts when the wheels were removed.

The four men – Burke, Wills, John King and
Charlie Gray – set off back to Cooper's Creek with
only half the supplies they needed. Storms lashed
the explorers and turned the ground to mud. Burke
found Gray stealing food and a fight broke out.
Weak with exhaustion, the men were still 500 km
(310 miles) from Cooper's Creek. Then Gray died
crossing the Stony Desert and when the others
arrived in Cooper's Creek, the camp was empty.

Burke decided they should head for a cattle
station 240 km (149 miles) away. Now mad with fever,
they walked in circles through the waterless desert.
Aborigines helped them until Burke shot at them with
his pistol. When Wills was too weak to walk they left
him, promising to find help. Soon after, Burke died.

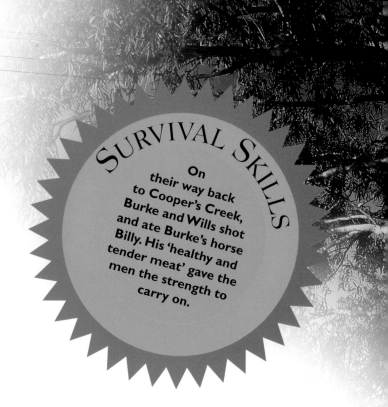

### SURVIVAL SKILLS

On
their way back
to Cooper's Creek,
Burke and Wills shot
and ate Burke's horse
Billy. His 'healthy and
tender meat' gave the
men the strength to
carry on.

▼ *Aborigines kept King alive until a search party found him
two months later, in September 1861.*

## FATAL MISTAKE

When the three survivors arrived at Cooper's Creek, they found a message carved on a tree: DIG 3FT. NW. APR. 21 1861. Burke dug up buried supplies – and a letter showing that the other men had left that very morning! Burke's party buried details of their planned route in the hope that someone might find them. However, they did not change the message on the tree. The main party came back to Cooper's Creek to double-check – but they had no reason to dig up the new letter.

▲ At first, Burke and the others tried to live off flour made from the nardoo plant and any animals they could shoot. In fact, eating nardoo reduces vitamin B in the body, making people more likely to get sick. If Burke had been a better bushman, the men could have survived on the fish living in Cooper's Creek.

When the three survivors arrived at Cooper's Creek Wills' legs were paralyzed.

Burke and Wills became national heroes and received state funerals.

Rival John McDouall Stuart reached the north coast in 1862 and claimed the prize.

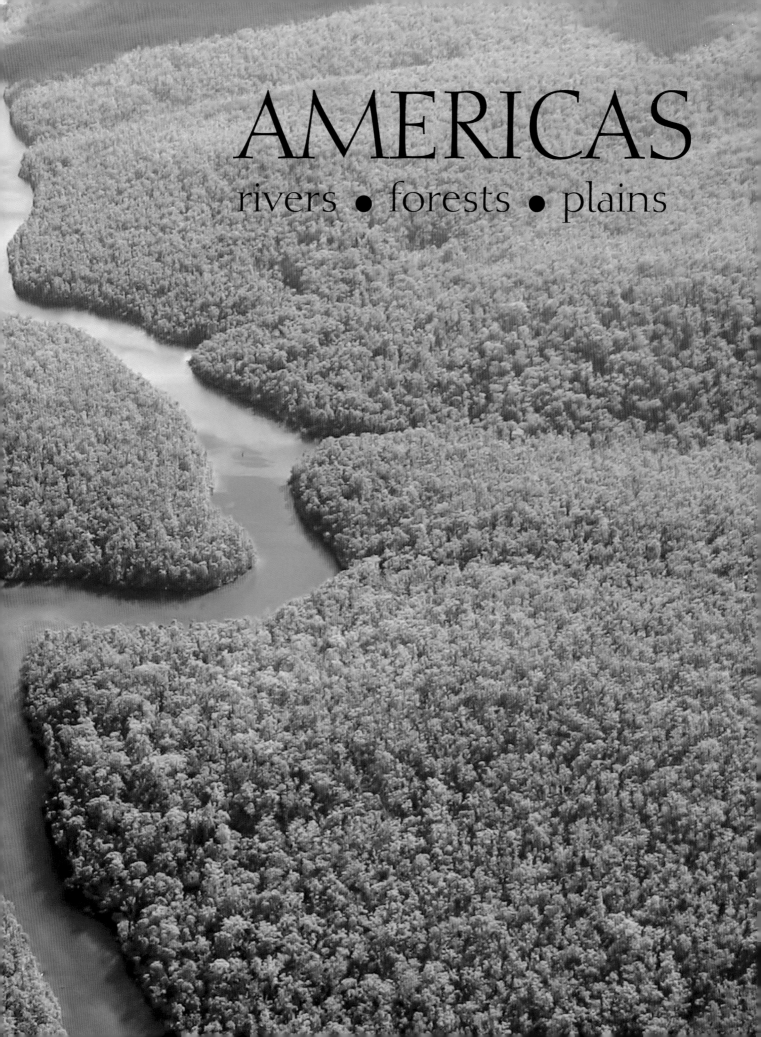

# AMERICAS

### rivers • forests • plains

# NORTH AMERICA OVERVIEW

TO REACH THE NEW WORLD, EUROPEAN SAILORS BRAVED STORMS AND ICEBERGS IN THE ATLANTIC. IN AMERICA, EXPLORERS FACED DESERTS, MOUNTAINS AND SWAMPS.

PEOPLE HAD LIVED IN AMERICA FOR 20,000 YEARS WHEN CHRISTOPHER COLUMBUS'S 'DISCOVERY' OF THE CONTINENT BEGAN A WAVE OF EXPLORATION.

Gold-hungry Spanish and French explorers found little treasure but opened up routes into the Southwest and into Canada. Europeans settled on the East Coast, but it was only in 1805 that an expedition crossed the Rockies to the Pacific. The journey blazed a trail for the wagon trains of European settlers.

## LOOK CLOSER

Many native peoples saw Europeans as invaders, but others welcomed them. Having a good interpreter could make the difference between life and death for an expedition.

## WHY GO THERE?

- **TRADE:** *Early explorers were looking for sea routes to East Asia. Later, mountain men travelled inland hunting animals for fur.*

- **GOLD:** *Spanish and French explorers were lured by stories of wealthy cities: none existed.*

- **LAND:** *Settlers arrived from the 17th century onwards, pushing native peoples west.*

- **RELIGION:** *Many early settlers were Christian pilgrims who hoped to start a new life where they could practise their religion freely.*

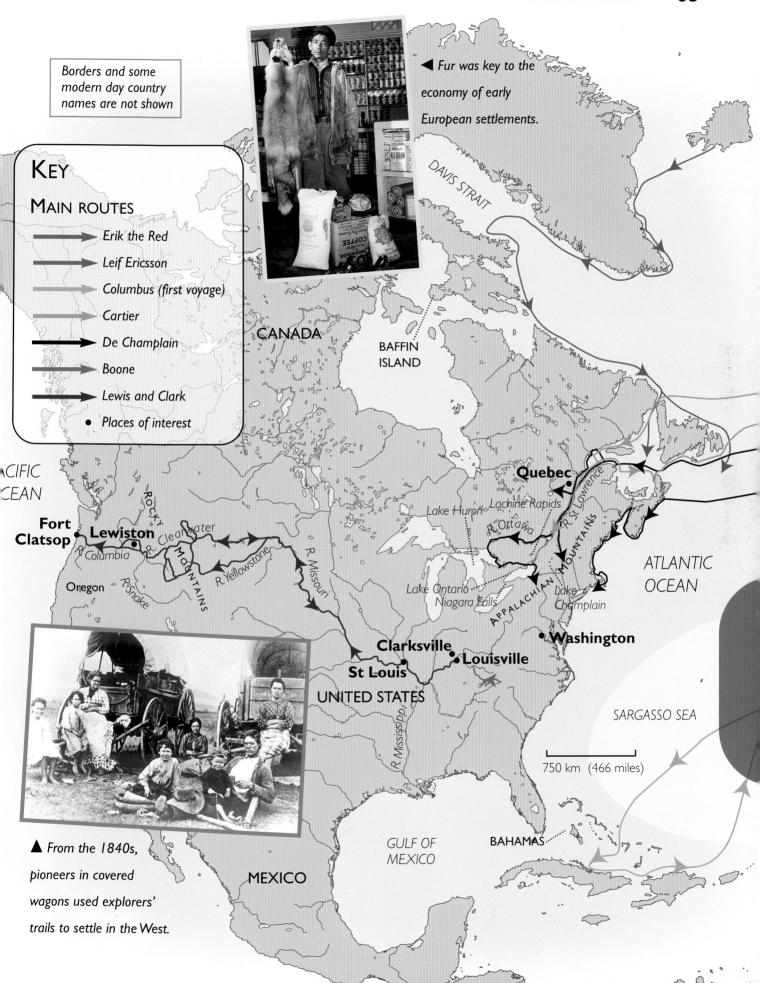

Borders and some modern day country names are not shown

# KEY

## MAIN ROUTES

Erik the Red

Leif Ericsson

Columbus (first voyage)

Cartier

De Champlain

Boone

Lewis and Clark

• Places of interest

◀ Fur was key to the economy of early European settlements.

DAVIS STRAIT

CANADA

BAFFIN ISLAND

PACIFIC OCEAN

ROCKY MOUNTAINS

Fort Clatsop • **Lewiston**

R. Columbia

R. Clearwater

Oregon

R. Snake

R. Yellowstone

R. Missouri

**Quebec**

Lachine Rapids

R. St Lawrence

Lake Huron

R. Ottawa

APPALACHIAN MOUNTAINS

Lake Ontario

Niagara Falls

Lake Champlain

ATLANTIC OCEAN

**Clarksville**

**St Louis**

**Louisville**

• **Washington**

UNITED STATES

R. Mississippi

SARGASSO SEA

750 km (466 miles)

GULF OF MEXICO

BAHAMAS

MEXICO

▲ From the 1840s, pioneers in covered wagons used explorers' trails to settle in the West.

# LEIF ERICSSON 'THE LUCKY'

THE VIKINGS WERE A QUARRELSOME BUNCH. IN 980, TROUBLEMAKER ERIC THE RED WAS BANISHED FROM ICELAND FOR THREE YEARS. HE SAILED WEST, ARRIVING IN WHAT IS NOW GREENLAND.

When he returned to Iceland six years later, Eric persuaded others to follow in his footsteps, including his son Leif Ericsson. Some time in the years after 1000, Leif crossed over the Davis Strait from Greenland and headed south. First he landed in a wild, rocky place now known as Baffin Island in Canada. Then he came to the island we call Newfoundland and became the first European known to have reached America. He and his men spent the winter there. Then, sailing farther south along the coast, they found a place where wild grapes grew, so they named it 'wineland' or Vinland. When spring came, they headed home.

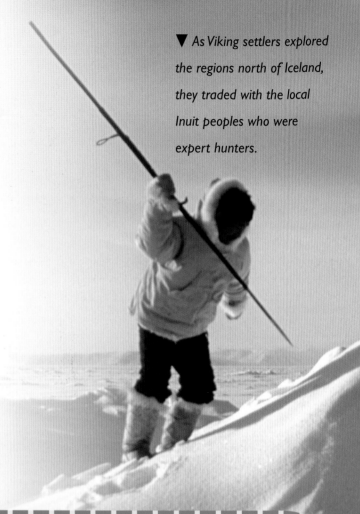

▼ As Viking settlers explored the regions north of Iceland, they traded with the local Inuit peoples who were expert hunters.

### SAINT BRENDAN "THE BOLD"

In the 6th century CE, the Irish monk Brendan set off from Ireland in a currah, a small ship made from leather, to spread the Christian word. He sailed west and, during the seven-year voyage, may have reached North America. On his return, Saint Brendan wrote about his adventure, describing the 'floating ice palaces' or icebergs he saw in the North Atlantic and 'mountains in the sea spouting fire', which may have been volcanoes in either Iceland or the Canary Islands.

◄ No-one knows how far or where Saint Brendan travelled, but at this time other brave monks did make dangerous sea voyages across the Atlantic.

▲ *The Vikings sailed in longships, wooden boats that could survive in the roughest seas. When rowing, the crew sat on sea chests containing their possessions. Warriors hung their shields on the sides of the boat.*

## SURVIVAL SKILLS

To navigate, Vikings watched birds and the wind's direction and speed. They also used magnetic stones that pointed north when floated on wood in water, just like a compass.

Name: Leif Ericsson

Born: 971, Iceland

Died: 1015, Iceland

Notable achievements: Leif Ericsson was the first European known to sail to America. As a boy, he heard about Bjarni Herjulfsson, who had seen the coast of Newfoundland. So Leif's discovery of America was no accident. He set sail from Greenland, passing Baffin Island and the Labrador coast. In Newfoundland, Leif's men loaded their ships with timber. Leif did so well from selling the wood back in Iceland that he was nicknamed 'Lucky'. He never returned to Vinland, perhaps due to the failure of other expeditions and the death of his brother, Thorvald, who was killed by Native Americans.

# CHRISTOPHER COLUMBUS

WHEN THE ITALIAN MARINER CHRISTOPHER COLUMBUS RODE THROUGH THE STREETS OF BARCELONA IN APRIL 1493, THE SPANISH CROWDS CHEERED. THEY BELIEVED HE HAD DISCOVERED A NEW ROUTE TO ASIA THAT WOULD MAKE THEIR COUNTRY RICH.

Yet Columbus hadn't done this at all. Instead, he'd stumbled on America. Columbus was one in a long line of sailors who tried to reach China by sailing west across the Atlantic Ocean.

Sponsored by King Ferdinand and Queen Isabella, in August 1492 Columbus had set out with a crew of 90 and three ships – the *Niña*, *Pinta* and *Santa María*. Two months later, Columbus sighted land – an island in the Caribbean where the local Arawak people flocked to the shore to greet him. Columbus called them 'Indians' as he was sure he had reached Asia, or the 'Indies' as it was then called.

## LOOK CLOSER

Columbus measured his ship's progress with a plank floating in the water. Using this method he knew he had covered 5,000 km (3,108 miles) in 33 days.

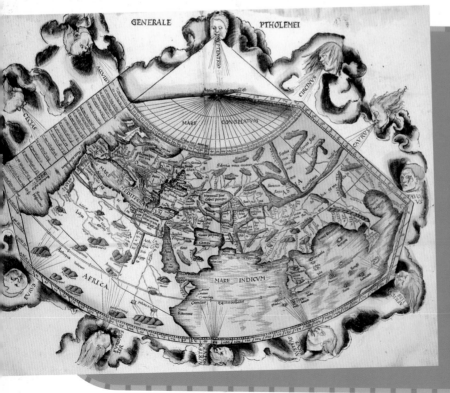

## FAR FAR AWAY

Like most people of this time, Columbus relied on maps made by the ancient Greek geographer Ptolemy. These made Asia appear much closer to Europe than it is. If Columbus had known the real width of the Atlantic Ocean, he might never have set out on his voyage!

◀ Ptolemy (127–145 CE) estimated that the Earth was much smaller than it really is, so the maps he drew look distorted today.

Name: Christopher Columbus

Born: 1451, Genoa, Italy

Died: 20 May, 1506,

Valladolid, Spain

Notable achievements: In 1492, Christopher Columbus (known as Cristoforo Colombo in Italian) sailed from Spain across the Atlantic Ocean, landing on an island in the Bahamas. This voyage led to 300 years of exploration in the Americas. After returning to Europe to spread the news, Columbus set off again in September 1493, this time with 17 ships and 1,200 men. He founded the first European town in the New World, La Isabela, in what is now the Dominican Republic. On his third expedition (1498-1500), Columbus landed on the coast of Venezuela, becoming the first European to set foot on the South American mainland. In his fourth expedition (1502-1504) he sailed along the coasts of what are now Jamaica, Honduras and Nicaragua (all in Central America), still looking for that elusive route to East Asia.

In his younger days, Columbus' ship was attacked and sunk off Portugal.

He found work in Lisbon and a few years later sailed as far as Iceland and West Africa.

After reading about Marco Polo's travels he decided to find a new sea route to Asia.

▶ Columbus named the island he landed on in the Bahamas San Salvador, although the people who lived there called it Guanahani.

For three months, Columbus' men explored the Caribbean islands looking for gold to trade. They found it on the island of Hispaniola (now divided between Haiti and the Dominican Republic). Then, on Christmas Eve in 1492, the *Santa María* was wrecked on the north coast of the island. Leaving 39 crew behind to trade for more gold, Columbus hurriedly set sail for Europe with the *Niña* and *Pinta*. When Columbus finally made it back to Spain, he received a hero's welcome and was given the title 'Admiral of the Oceans'.

▼ *Columbus brought back gold, parrots, spices and captives from his first expedition to persuade King Ferdinand and Queen Isabella to back his next voyage.*

Columbus was convinced that he had found a new route to Asia. He made three more journeys to the Americas to prove he was right. He wasn't, but his mistake changed the course of history forever.

> It took Columbus eight years to persuade Queen Isabella to fund his voyages.

> Without a royal sponsor it was impossible to make any claims to new-found lands.

> After the discoveries, Columbus had to beg for the titles and money promised him.

LOOK CLOSER

Columbus was lucky that the Taino people he met in the Caribbean were friendly. When the *Santa María* ran aground, a local chief, Guacanagari, sent canoes to rescue him.

▶ *The Santa María had 40 crew and was armed with cannons that fired stone balls. After it ran aground, its planks were used to build a fort.*

▲ Caribbean islanders welcomed European explorers, but 260,000 people died in 15 years of diseases carried by the newcomers.

## COLUMBUS IN AMERICA

When Columbus returned to the island of Hispaniola in 1494, he discovered that the crew he had left behind had been killed. Chief Caonabo, leader of the Carib peoples living on the island, had caught the Spanish settlers kidnapping women and stealing gold. In January 1494, the colonists of Columbus's new colony at La Isabela on Dominica, also began looting from local people. The colonists here also began looting from local people. Spanish settlers criticized Columbus' government of the colony. In 1500, he was sent back to Spain in chains to report to Queen Isabella.

# JACQUES CARTIER

FRENCHMAN JACQUES CARTIER SET OUT ACROSS THE ATLANTIC IN 1534 HOPING TO 'DISCOVER ISLANDS WHERE GOLD AND OTHER PRECIOUS THINGS ARE TO BE FOUND'.

In 1544, he sailed up the St Lawrence River, setting up camp near to what is now Quebec. Here Cartier pestered the local Iroquois with questions about gold and gems, so they made up a story about the fabulously rich 'Kingdom of Saguenay' further inland. Cartier set out to look for it, but his ships stopped at the thundering Lachine rapids. Cartier kidnapped 10 Iroquois and returned to France. Their stories of Saguenay persuaded the French king to back Cartier's next expedition in 1541.

Cartier returned to Canada with 700 settlers, but the diamonds and gold he found there turned out to be worthless.

Name: Jacques Cartier
Born: 31 December, 1491, Saint-Malo, France
Died: 1 September, 1557, Saint-Malo, France
Notable achievements: Cartier never found the gold he had hoped for. However, he was the first European to explore the interior of Canada and, unlike Columbus, he realized that America was a new continent, not part of Asia. Cartier was a skilled navigator. On his first expedition he crossed the Atlantic in just 20 days. His three voyages to North America produced important maps of the area around the St Lawrence River, to which he first gave the name 'Canada'. However, the colonies set up by Cartier all failed. It was 150 years before more settlers arrived.

▼ Ships still get trapped when the St Lawrence River freezes. In the winter of 1535–1536, ice up to 1.8 m (6 ft) thick stopped the French fleet getting supplies to Cartier's party.

▲ *Cartier was guided around the St Lawrence region by the Iroquois who lived there – but he repaid their help by kidnapping some of them to take back to France.*

## SURVIVAL SKILLS

During a bad winter, scurvy almost killed Cartier's men. They were saved by the Iroquois who made them a drink from the bark of white cedar trees, which is rich in Vitamin C.

## CROSS COUNTRY

Scottish fur trader Alexander Mackenzie (1755–1820) followed in the footsteps of Cartier when, in 1793, he became the first European to cross North America. Mackenzie voyaged 1,000 km (622 miles) down the Peace and Fraser rivers, where his canoe was wrecked in rapids and he almost drowned. Hostile Native Americans prevented him reaching the Pacific, even though he could see it, and Mackenzie turned back having painted a rock with the words: 'From Canada by land 22nd July 1793'.

# SAMUEL DE CHAMPLAIN

A FORMER SOLDIER AND SEA CAPTAIN, FRENCHMAN SAMUEL DE CHAMPLAIN WENT TO CANADA TO SET UP A FUR TRADING COLONY AND EXPLORE BEYOND THE MIGHTY LACHINE RAPIDS ON THE ST LAWRENCE RIVER.

After charting the Atlantic coastline and building a fort at Quebec, he finally got the chance to explore inland. In 1609, he joined a war party of the local Huron people, who showed him Lake Champlain.

Champlain realized he could learn a lot from the Huron. When in 1613 he received a grant to take over the fur trade in Canada, he paddled north up the Ottawa River to Allumette Island. Two years later he joined another Huron raid against the Iroquois. This time he reached Lake Huron, returning via Lake Ontario.

Champlain asked the Huron questions through an interpreter.

From them he worked out the network of the Great Lakes, including the Niagara Falls.

Champlain later sent other explorers to chart the five lakes.

## HURON HELPERS

In September 1615, during a Huron raid, Champlain got hit in the knee by an Iroquois arrow. Unable to walk, he was carried to the Huron settlement on the back of a Huron warrior. Champlain was forced to spend the winter there. Restless as ever, he used the time to visit neighbouring tribes and took notes about their way of life.

► The Huron traded beaver and martin furs with the French, in return for guns, blankets, beads and jewellery.

▲ *The name 'Quebec' means 'strait' or 'narrows'. Champlain named the city because it stood at a place where the St Lawrence River narrows to flow through a cliff-lined gap.*

## LOOK CLOSER

Champlain saw that the Huron could carry their canoes around the rapids. He realized Indian canoes were perfect for travelling through the forests of north-eastern America.

Name: Samuel de Champlain
Born: 1567, Brouage, France
Died: 1635, Quebec, New France (now Canada)

Notable achievements:
Champlain was the real founder of Canada. Over 20 years, he made 21 voyages across the Atlantic to explore the region. From 1604-1607, Champlain made excellent charts of the Atlantic coast as far south as Cape Cod. In 1608, he founded Quebec with 32 other settlers (though nearly three-quarters of them died during the first winter). He discovered Lake Champlain in 1609 and also explored the Ottawa River and the eastern Great Lakes. Champlain's books and charts, maps and route plans were the first detailed study of Canada.

# DANIEL BOONE

Growing up on the Pennsylvania frontier, Daniel Boone fell in love with the wilderness. As a boy, he tracked animals through the woods with a home-made spear.

Later, Boone met John Finley, an old hunter bursting with tales of the western wilds. In 1769, he and his brother joined Finley's group and set out along the Warrior's Path into Kentucky.

A few years later, Boone's troubles began. In 1773, his son was murdered. In 1776, the Shawnee and Cherokee captured his daughter Jemima. Boone rescued her but was himself captured by Shawnee two years later. He escaped and was robbed while heading east with settlers' money. He was cheated out of his land, and had to work as a surveyor before he settled in Spanish Louisiana (now Missouri) in 1799.

Name: Daniel Boone

Born: 2 November, 1734, Berks County, Pennsylvania, USA

Died: 26 September, 1820, St. Charles, USA

Notable achievement: Boone was a hunter and explorer whose exploits made him one of the most famous frontiersmen in American history. Boone's biggest achievement was exploring west into Kentucky during the 1760s and 70s. In 1775, Boone blazed a trail across the Appalachian Mountains through the Cumberland Gap. His party helped to build the Wilderness Road, which soon became a highway to the region then known as 'the West'. In 1784, John Filson wrote down Boone's story and made him into a folk hero. Boone was a brave and skilful woodsman who once said: 'I have never been lost, but I will admit to being confused for several weeks.'

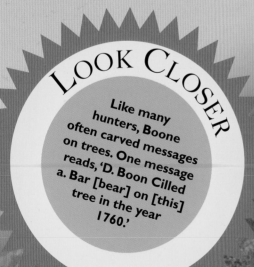

## LOOK CLOSER

Like many hunters, Boone often carved messages on trees. One message reads, 'D. Boon Cilled a. Bar [bear] on [this] tree in the year 1760.'

## DANGEROUS BUSINESS

Boone was not the only fur trapper to find new routes across North America. In the early 19th century, men such as Jedediah Smith (1799–1831) opened up the West. Smith was the first man to cross the Rocky Mountains into California. This was dangerous terrain: in 1823, Smith was nearly killed by a bear.

◀ *After Jedediah Smith was attacked by a bear, a fellow trapper had to sew his ear back on.*

▼ *Thousands of settlers followed Boone's trail through the Cumberland Gap across the Appalachian Mountains to make new homes on America's western frontier. Boone was at home in the Wilderness: he often went on hunting trips that lasted weeks or months, living in the mountains.*

Boone's daughter Jemima married one of the men who rescued her from the Shawnee.

After capturing Boone, the Shawnee's Chief Blackfish adopted him as his son.

# LEWIS AND CLARK

WHEN PRESIDENT JEFFERSON BOUGHT THE TERRITORY OF LOUISIANA FROM FRANCE IN 1803, HE ASKED EXPERT FRONTIERSMAN MERIWETHER LEWIS TO LEAD AN EXPEDITION ACROSS HIS NEW LANDS.

Lewis and his old army friend William Clark put together a team, and in 1804 the so-called Corps of Discovery set off from St Louis, heading up the Missouri River. It was a struggle pulling three boats against the current, yet by the end of the year the party had travelled 2,575 km (1,600 miles).

After spending the winter with the Mandan Sioux, the men hauled their boats upstream for another 1,610 km (1,000 miles). Here members of the Shoshone tribe gave them horses and a guide, but the party got trapped in deep snows in the Bitterroot Mountains. They only survived when they were given food by the friendly Nez Percé tribe.

## LOOK CLOSER

Clark made a special fold-up boat, the *Experiment*, to carry around the rapids. However, the boat wasn't water-tight, so Clark was forced to use canoes.

## A HELPING HAND

During the winter of 1804–1805, the expedition stayed with the Mandan. There they met the trapper Touissant Charbonneau and his Shoshone wife, Sacagawea. Charbonneau became the group's guide and Sacagawea their interpreter. The presence of Sacagawea and her baby son helped establish good relations with native peoples. In one Shoshone village, Sacagawea recognized the chief as her own brother!

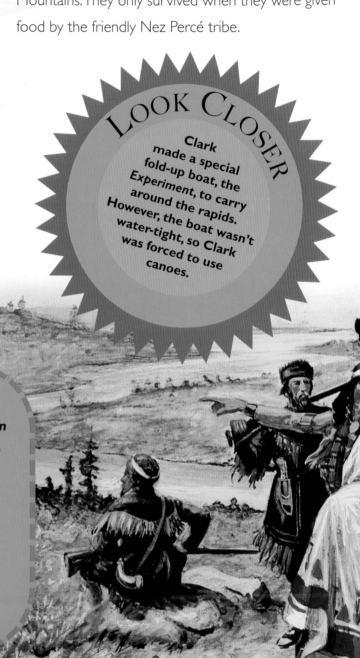

▶ Sacagawea was skilled at making medicines from plants; she also made moccasins for the explorers.

▲ The expedition's horses stumbled and slipped as they crossed the icy Bitterroot Mountains. The Bitterroots are part of the Rocky Mountains, the long mountain chain that divides North America.

Name: Meriwether Lewis
Born: 18 August, 1774, Virginia, British North America
Died: 11 October, 1809, Tennessee, USA

Name: William Clark
Born: 1 August, 1770, Virginia, British North America
Died: 1 September, 1838, St Louis, Missouri, USA

Notable achievement: In 1804, Lewis and Clark led the first expedition across America to the Pacific coast and back. They travelled over 14,485 km (9,000 miles) in 28 months. Six of the party kept journals of their trip. The expedition also brought back maps, animal skins, five caged birds and a prairie dog. Lewis and Clark's expedition also confirmed that there was no 'Northwest Passage' – an easy water crossing of the continent that would give fur traders a short-cut to markets in Asia.

▶ The Native Americans used dugout canoes to travel along the rivers. The canoes were made by hollowing out whole tree trunks, and could be up to 196 m (60 ft) long.

After their narrow escape in the Bitterroot Mountains, Lewis and Clark's party built new canoes and floated down the Clearwater, Snake and Columbia Rivers, braving white water rapids on the way. On 7 November 1805, they finally reached the Pacific coast where the party built a camp, named Fort Clatsop after a local tribe. They spent the winter there, then, in March, set out on the return journey.

▼ *The Columbia River that carried Lewis and Clark to the Pacific Ocean is 2,000 km (1,243 miles) long. The lower part of the river has many rapids, which made it a risky route for the settlers who later used it to head west toward Oregon.*

During the journey home, Lewis divided the expedition into small groups. He wanted to explore the Marias River further north. However, during the detour, Lewis' group met hostile Blackfoot warriors. They fled 145 km (90 miles) across the plains to join up with the rest of the party.

In September 1806, Lewis and Clark finally arrived back in St Louis where they were greeted as heroes. The US government gave them 6 km² (1,600 acres) of land as a reward for their exploits.

As well as native tribes, Lewis and Clark met trappers and hunters from Canada.

They had to avoid parties from the south, sent by the Spanish to intercept them.

Lewis identified 178 plants that were unknown to science, and 122 animals.

◀ *Lewis and Clark's party were the first Europeans to identify the grizzly bear. They became very familiar with the new species – they met no fewer than 62 grizzlies on the expedition!*

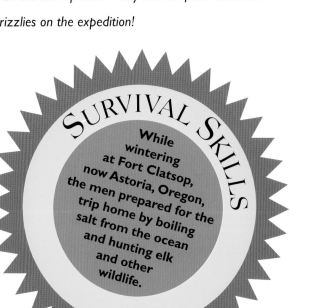

## SURVIVAL SKILLS

While wintering at Fort Clatsop, now Astoria, Oregon, the men prepared for the trip home by boiling salt from the ocean and hunting elk and other wildlife.

## ROUTE TO FREEDOM

The Corps of Discovery included Clark's slave York, an African American. During the expedition, York enjoyed relative freedom and was a valued member of the party. He was a big, strong man who impressed the Native Americans the expedition met. They had never seen an African American before. On one occasion York risked his life to save Clark and Sacagawea's family during a flash flood on the Missouri River. When the party got back to St Louis, York asked Clark to grant him his freedom so that he could join his wife. Clark eventually agreed – but not until ten years later.

▶ *York (kneeling) was about the same age as William Clark and, as Clark's father's slave, had been the explorer's companion since his early childhood.*

ONLY 100 YEARS AGO, AN EXPEDITION COULD DISAPPEAR WITHOUT TRACE IN THE AMAZON! EARLY EXPLORERS SCALED THE ANDES AND USED RIVERS TO PENETRATE THROUGH THICK JUNGLE.

# CENTRAL AND SOUTH AMERICA OVERVIEW

IN THE LATE 15TH CENTURY, FERDINAND MAGELLAN AND OTHER EUROPEANS USED STEADY WINDS TO CROSS THE ATLANTIC AND EXPLORE THE COAST OF SOUTH AMERICA.

The 16th century was the time of the 'conquistadors', Spanish soldiers, led by Hernán Cortés and Francisco Pizarro, who conquered the huge Aztec and Inca empires in Mexico and Peru. From Peru, the Spaniards explored deep into Colombia, Bolivia and Chile.

Fortune hunters such as Francisco de Orellana flocked to the New World. They used local guides or relied on sheer luck to find their way around. In the 19th century, scientific explorers discovered the source of the mighty river systems that led to the Atlantic coast.

## WHY GO THERE?

- **CONQUEST:** *Conquistadors – 'conquerors' – used superior technology and local allies to defeat the empires of the Aztec and Inca.*
- **GOLD:** *Fortune hunters searched for the land of the fabled El Dorado, the 'Golden Man'.*
- **RELIGION:** *Monks came to South America to convert the local peoples to Christianity.*
- **ARCHAEOLOGY:** *Later visitors explored ancient Maya and Inca ruins.*

XICO
**Tenochtitlán**
**Cholula**
**Veracruz**
**Acapulco**
COZUMEL
**Havana**
**Santiago de Cuba**
*SARGASSO SEA*

1000 km (621 miles)

**Cartagena**
**Panama**
**Caracas**
**Cumana**
VENEZUELA
*R. Orinoco*
*R. Orinoco*
**Bogotá**
COLOMBIA

GORGONA ISLAND

▲ *Traces of Tenochtitlán,
the Aztec capital, can still
be seen in parts of
modern-day Mexico City.*

**Quito**
*R. Napo*
ECUADOR
**Tumbes**
*R. Negro*
**Piura**
*R. Amazon*
*R. Amazon*
**Cajamarca**
*R. Madeira*
BRAZIL
PERU
PACIFIC
OCEAN

Borders and some
modern day country
names are not shown

ANDES MOUNTAINS
**Lima**
**Cuzco**
BOLIVIA

*Lake Titicaca*

## LOOK CLOSER

Explorers
faced dangerous
animals such as
alligators, snakes,
jaguars and piranhas. The
worst threat was often
human. Explorers were
killed by native tribes
– or by their own
men!

## KEY

### MAIN ROUTES      OTHERS

⟶ *Pizarro*      ┈┈➤

⟶ *Orellana*

⟶ *Cortés*

⟶ *Humboldt*

• *Places of interest*

▶ *Maya cities, such as Palenque in Mexico,
were home to many people but declined and
were abandoned after the Europeans arrived.*

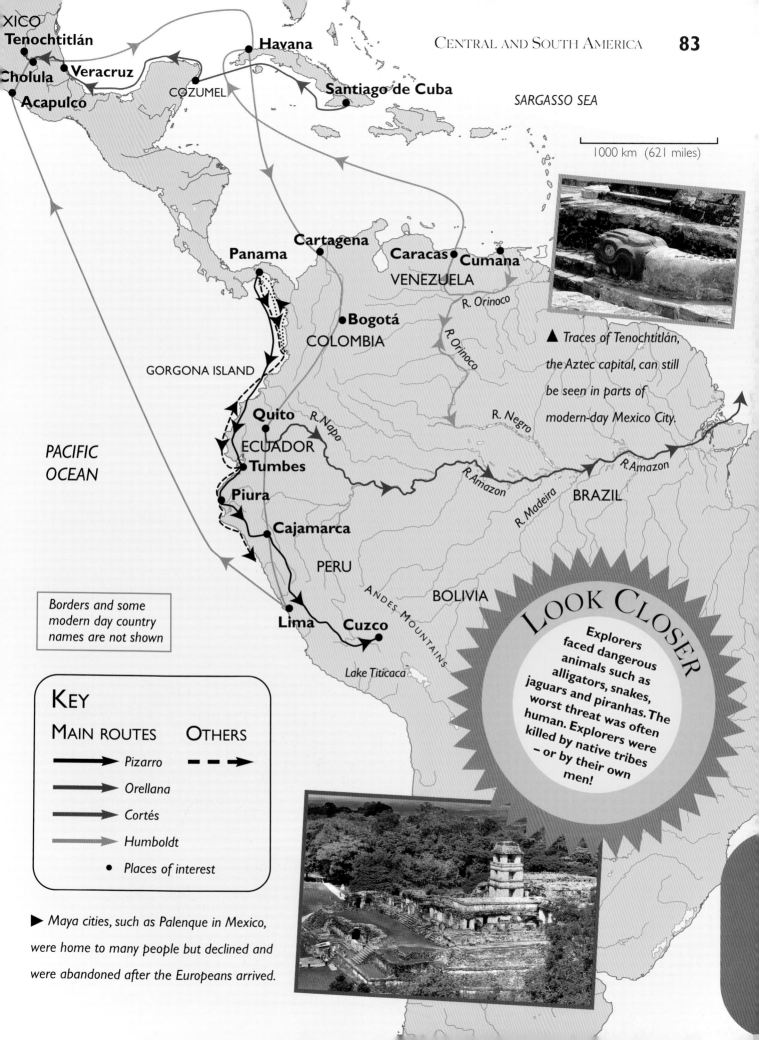

# HERNÁN CORTÉS

H ERNÁN CORTÉS WAS A TROUBLE-MAKER, SO THE GOVERNOR OF CUBA DECIDED TO SEND HIM TO MEXICO. THEN HE CHANGED HIS MIND.

'Too late!' thought Cortés who, on 18 February, 1519, landed on Mexico's southeast coast and joined forces with the local Tlaxcala people, who hated their Aztec rulers. With 6,000 men under his command, Cortés marched to Tenochtitlán, the Aztec capital.

There, the Aztec emperor Moctezuma invited Cortés into the city. Cortés took the emperor hostage, but hearing that a rival Spanish force was on its way, left his men in charge and returned to the coast to win them over. Back in Tenochtitlán, he found his men had provoked an Aztec revolt. Cortés led his troops away but returned in 1521 to conquer the city, and with it the Aztec empire.

Name: Hernán Cortés

Born: 1485, Medellín, Spain

Died: 2 December, 1547, Castilleja de la Cuesta (near Seville), Spain

Notable achievement: Hernán Cortés explored and conquered Aztec Mexico for Spain in less than two years. The siege of Tenochtitlán lasted 75 days and left the city in ruins. This battle and the spread of European diseases, such as smallpox, killed 240,000 Aztecs. When he was made governor of the conquered region, Cortés rebuilt Tenochtitlán as the Spanish city of Mexico. Within a short time he had conquered many of the neighbouring peoples, but he ruled over his new empire with great cruelty. A few years later, in 1524, he was forced to retire.

## CRUEL CONQUEST

The Aztecs were terrifying neighbours. Every year they captured tens of thousands of victims for sacrifice, ripping out their hearts and displaying their heads in wooden racks. However, Cortés' men could also be brutal. Horses helped them move quickly and their iron swords sliced through the Aztecs' wooden shields.

◀ When Cortés and his men entered the town of Cholula, they slaughtered 5,000 people.

## LOOK CLOSER

Cortés was arrogant, ruthless and cunning, but also a skilful and strong leader. He was able to inspire a crew of soldiers, fortune hunters and tradesmen to follow him.

▲ Skull racks, or tzompantli, were used by the Aztecs to display the skulls of sacrificial victims. One rack contained the heads of Spaniards and their horses, intended as a warning to Cortés.

► Few of the pyramids the Aztecs used for rituals survive. The arrival of the Spaniards began a process in which the pyramids were pulled down or had other structures built on top of them.

# FRANCISCO PIZARRO

Francisco Pizarro arrived in the New World in 1502. For over 20 years he fought brutal wars against the local peoples of the Caribbean and Panama.

Pizarro left Panama in December 1530. He landed in Ecuador and spent a year hacking through jungle and fighting tribes before crossing the mountains into Peru – a journey of 2,500 km (1,554 miles).

When the Inca king, Atahualpa, went to greet the Spaniards, Pizarro launched a surprise attack. He later executed Atahualpa. In November 1533, Pizarro entered the Inca capital, Cuzco. In less than a year he had conquered the enormous Inca empire.

## GATE OF HELL

On his second expedition (1526–1528), Pizarro landed on the island of Gorgona, the 'gate of hell', where his men began dying of disease and hunger. He asked the Governor of Panama to send provisions. When none arrived, Pizarro is said to have drawn a line in the sand, daring his men to cross it. He promised glory and gold to anyone who stayed with him. Only 13 of the 80 men accepted his offer; the rest fled to return home.

▼ Pizarro's men never found the mountain-top city of Machu Picchu, the most famous symbol of the Inca empire. Situated about 80 km (50 miles) north of Cuzco, it remained undiscovered until 1911.

▲ When Pizarro (on horseback in this picture) captured King Atahualpa (shown on his throne), he was offered a room filled with gold and silver to release the king. Pizarro accepted the treasure, then broke his promise and killed the king anyway.

## SURVIVAL SKILLS

Pizarro's key tactic was surprise. When he first met Atahualpa at Cajamarca, he launched a sudden attack during a ceremonial parade. In two hours, his small force killed 7,000 Inca.

Name: Francisco Pizarro

Born: 1475, Trujillo, Spain

Died: 26 June, 1541, Lima (now in Peru)

Notable achievement: Conquistador Francisco Pizarro's main claim to fame is his conquest of the Inca empire in Peru with just 168 men. By a stroke of luck, he arrived during a civil war between Atahualpa and his brother Huascar, which greatly weakened the Inca. After founding the city of Lima in 1535, Pizarro fought with a rival conquistador Diego de Almagro. Pizarro's brother Hernando had Almagro executed in 1538, but three years later Pizarro was killed by Almagro's supporters.

# FRANCISCO DE ORELLANA

**A**LTHOUGH CONQUISTADOR FRANCISCO DE ORELLANA HAD JUST TAKEN PART IN THE CONQUEST OF THE INCA EMPIRE, HE WAS STILL HUNGRY FOR GOLD.

Orellana joined Gonzalo Pizarro, half-brother of Francisco Pizarro, to search for the legendary 'Land of Cinnamon'. In March 1541, 280 men left Quito in Peru. They struggled over mountains and through jungle. By October they were out of food.

The men built a boat, and Orellana led a group to search downstream for supplies. They found a village after 12 days, but by then Orellana's men were too weak to row back upriver. Under attack from war canoes and archers on the river banks, they could only drift with the current. Eight months and 8,000 km (4,972 miles) later, in August 1542, Orellana's men arrived at the Atlantic Ocean. They had travelled down the world's greatest river, the Amazon.

## LOOK CLOSER

Orellana named the Amazon River after a tribe of fierce female warriors he fought during his journey. They reminded him of the Amazons of ancient Greek mythology.

Name: Francisco de Orellana
Born: 1490, Trujillo, Spain
Died: 1546, Amazon River, Brazil
Notable achievement: Francisco de Orellana was the first European to travel down the Amazon River. He arrived in the New World as a teenager and later lost his eye fighting the Inca during the conquest of the Inca empire. After his voyage down the Amazon, Orellana returned to Spain. There he was rewarded with a title and sent to colonise the Amazon region. Orellana returned with hundreds of settlers, but died when his ship sank in the Amazon delta.

▲ *The Amazon is the second-longest river in the world after the Nile. After his remarkable journey down the Amazon, Orellana was welcomed back to Spain as a hero — but Gonzalo Pizarro insisted that he was a traitor for not returning to help the original expedition.*

During the trip, Orellana's boat was hit by so many arrows it 'looked like a porcupine'.

Orellana learned enough words along the Amazon to trade beads and trinkets for food.

Meanwhile, Gonzalo Pizarro's men took nine months to get back to Quito.

## FISH OUT OF WATER

Spanish soldiers may have been the best fighters in Europe, but they didn't know how to find food in the jungle. Orellana's men were so hungry they ate their horses and dogs and finally their own shoes cooked with herbs. Seven men died of hunger before Orellana was helped by the heavy rains. In eight days, the strong current swept his boat 1,200 km (746 miles) downstream.

► *Orellana made a mistake by trying to cut a path through the jungle rather than travelling along its rivers.*

# ALEXANDER VON HUMBOLDT

I N 1799, ALEXANDER VON HUMBOLDT BEGAN AN INCREDIBLE JOURNEY THAT TOOK HIM FROM SPAIN ACROSS THE ATLANTIC TO SOUTH AMERICA AND THEN NORTH TO THE UNITED STATES.

Humboldt set off with botanist Aimé Bonpland and in June they arrived in Venezuela. They explored the region around the Orinoco River. When rains and insects destroyed their supplies, they lived off wild cacao beans and river water. They got sick but recovered, and in November they sailed to Cuba.

Six months later the pair trekked along the Andes. In 1803 they headed north to Mexico, where they explored the country for a year and climbed a volcano. Turning for home, they stopped off in the United States before arriving back in France in August 1804. Phew!

Name: Alexander von Humboldt
Born: 14 September, 1769, Berlin, Prussia (now Germany)
Died: 6 May, 1859, Berlin
Notable achievements: From 1799 to 1804, Alexander von Humboldt and French botanist Aimé Bonpland explored the coast of Venezuela, the Amazon and Orinoco Rivers, and much of Peru, Ecuador, Colombia and Mexico. They travelled over 9,600 km (5,966 miles) on foot, on horseback and in canoes. As well as important discoveries about the local wildlife and geology, Humbolt made the link between the Amazon and Orinoco river systems. Between them, Humboldt and Bonpland published many books.

Humboldt and Bonpland endured crocodile-infested swamps, rapids and freezing cold.

At one stage, the pair were so low on food they were forced to eat ants.

They discovered the oilbird, which lives in caves and can find its way in the dark.

► Humboldt and Bonpland travelled with 40 pieces of scientific equipment that could measure everything from magnetic currents to how blue the sky was.

LOOK CLOSER

South America could be a dangerous place. Once, Humboldt was walking alone on a beach when he came face to face with a jaguar. Luckily, the big cat left him alone.

▼ In 1802 Humboldt and Bonpland climbed 6,005 m (19,700 ft) up Mount Chimborazo – a world mountain-climbing record for nearly 30 years!

## ANIMAL EXPERIMENTS

Humboldt and Bonpland wanted to study the electric eels that lived in the rivers of Venezuela. But catching the 2m- (7 ft-) long fish was risky – they could deliver a powerful 650-volt shock. With a local man, the pair came up with a plan. They would drive 30 horses and mules into the water and keep them there while the eels used up all their energy. The waters boiled as the yellow eels stung the struggling horses again and again. Eventually the eels ran out of power and Humboldt could catch them safely, but at the cost of two horses, which drowned.

# POLAR REGIONS

icebergs • mountains •
frozen deserts

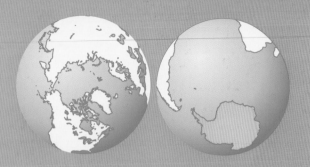

ANTARCTICA WAS

THE LAST

CONTINENT TO

BE EXPLORED. THE

COLDEST PLACE

ON EARTH, IT'S ALSO

THE WINDIEST,

HIGHEST,

DARKEST AND

LONELIEST.

# POLAR REGIONS OVERVIEW

NATIVE PEOPLES LIVED INSIDE THE ARCTIC CIRCLE FOR CENTURIES BEFORE EUROPEAN EXPLORERS SET OUT TO FIND SEA ROUTES AROUND THE EDGE OF THE FROZEN ARCTIC OCEAN AND TO REACH THE NORTH POLE.

In the south, explorers seeking the 'Great Southern Continent' discovered Antarctica in the early 19th century.

In 1827, English explorer Captain William Parry tried but failed to reach the North Pole by sled. In the early 20th century, Norwegian explorer Roald Amundsen learned how to use dogs and sleds from the Inuit. The Americans Robert Peary and Matthew Henson beat Amundsen to the North Pole in 1909. Amundsen set his sights on the South Pole – and the race with Englishman Robert Scott was on!

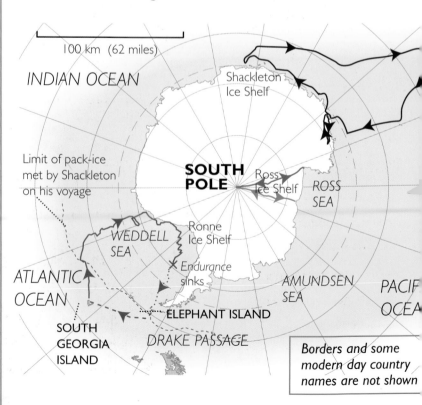

100 km (62 miles)

INDIAN OCEAN

Shackleton Ice Shelf

Limit of pack-ice met by Shackleton on his voyage

**SOUTH POLE**

Ross Ice Shelf

ROSS SEA

Ronne Ice Shelf

WEDDELL SEA

Endurance sinks

AMUNDSEN SEA

PACIFIC OCEAN

ATLANTIC OCEAN

ELEPHANT ISLAND

SOUTH GEORGIA ISLAND

DRAKE PASSAGE

Borders and some modern day country names are not shown

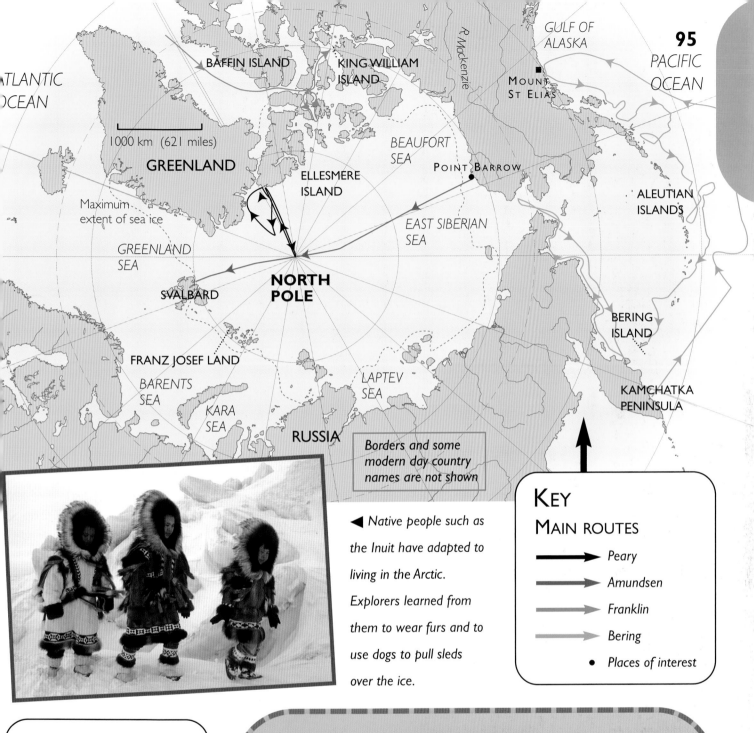

ATLANTIC OCEAN

BAFFIN ISLAND

KING WILLIAM ISLAND

R. Mackenzie

MOUNT ST ELIAS

1000 km (621 miles)

**GREENLAND**

ELLESMERE ISLAND

BEAUFORT SEA

POINT BARROW

ALEUTIAN ISLANDS

Maximum extent of sea ice

*GREENLAND SEA*

EAST SIBERIAN SEA

*SVALBARD*

**NORTH POLE**

BERING ISLAND

FRANZ JOSEF LAND

*BARENTS SEA*

*LAPTEV SEA*

KAMCHATKA PENINSULA

*KARA SEA*

**RUSSIA**

*Borders and some modern day country names are not shown*

◄ *Native people such as the Inuit have adapted to living in the Arctic. Explorers learned from them to wear furs and to use dogs to pull sleds over the ice.*

## KEY
### MAIN ROUTES

→ *Peary*

→ *Amundsen*

→ *Franklin*

→ *Bering*

● *Places of interest*

## KEY
### MAIN ROUTES

→ *Scott*

→ *Amundsen*

→ *Shackleton*

•••••► *(adrift on ice)*

‑ ‑ ‑► *(in open boat)*

→ *Mawson*

## WHY GO THERE?

● **THE POLES:** *Explorers wanted the glory of being the first to reach the ends of the world.*

● **TRADE:** *Traders hoped that the Northwest Passage, a water route around the top of Canada, would offer a short-cut to East Asia.*

● **SCIENCE:** *Expeditions took scientists to record the weather, take rock samples and study wildlife.*

● **IMPERIAL RIVALRY:** *Ten nations planned expeditions to the South Pole – but the final race was between Britain and Norway.*

# VITUS BERING

BERING WAS A DANISH NAVIGATOR WHO LED A RUSSIAN EXPEDITION TO FIND OUT WHETHER ASIA AND NORTH AMERICA WERE JOINED BY LAND.

In 1724, Bering's party set off across 10,000 km (6,215 miles) of Siberian wilderness to the Pacific coast. In 1728, Bering set sail from the Kamchatka Peninsula, but fog prevented him from seeing the coast of Alaska. After a month at sea, he turned back!

Bering was criticized for not going further, so in 1740 he set out again. It took him three years to cross Siberia, then a violent storm separated his two ships. Both explored the coast of Alaska, and the *St Paul* returned safely. The *St Peter*, on which Bering was travelling, got lost. Bering and his crew spent the winter on what is now Bering Island. Within three months, Bering and 29 of his crew were dead.

## ILL-FATED JOURNEY

On the journey home from Alaska in 1741, things went from bad to worse on board the St Peter. Bering lost his way, the barrels of drinking water began to leak and the food ran out. Many of the crew were struck by scurvy. Bering became too weak to leave his cabin. On 4 November, an island was sighted. With a damaged ship and a sick crew, Bering decided to spend the winter on the island. Though he grew weaker each day, he continued to lead his men until his death on 8 December, 1741.

When Bering became too ill to command his ship, he landed on what is now Bering Island.

Heavy snows there meant that Bering's party had to dig themselves out of their huts.

◀ *The St Peter ran aground on the rocky, foggy coast of Alaska. After Bering's death, survivors built small boats from the wreck of the St Peter and managed to reach the mainland of Siberia.*

## LOOK CLOSER

Heavy snows on the island meant that Bering's party were often unable to find the driftwood needed for fires. On some days they had to walk nearly 16 km (10 miles) to find it.

◀ *Bering crossed the strait separating Asia from America in 1728 as he looked for the Northeast Passage to China. The strait has since been named after him.*

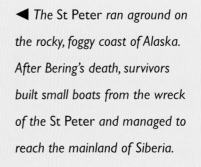

Name: **Vitus Jonassen Bering**
Born: **August, 1681, Horsens, Denmark**
Died: **19 December, 1741, Bering Island**
Notable achievements: **Danish by birth, Bering served in the Russian Navy. In his first expedition, he passed through the Bering Strait (named after him), proving that Asia and North America were separate continents - although he did not realize it. In his second expedition, Bering's two ships got separated. The** *St Paul* **sighted the coast of Alaska; Bering's crew saw Mount St Elias a few days later. Bering's voyages later led to Russia's Great Northern Expedition, which mapped the Arctic coast of Siberia from 1733 to 1743.**

# JOHN FRANKLIN

WHEN ENGLISHMAN JOHN FRANKLIN SAILED ALONG CANADA'S NORTHERN COASTLINE IN 1845, NO OTHER EUROPEAN EXPLORERS HAD BEEN WITHIN 800 KM (500 MILES) OF THESE UNCHARTED WATERS.

Franklin had previously crossed Canada from the Great Slave Lake to the Arctic coast (1819–1822). From 1825 to 1827, he mapped more of the Arctic coastline. In 1844, Franklin set out to find the Northwest Passage, a sea route from the Atlantic to the Pacific through the Arctic islands of northern Canada. When there was no word from him after three years, search parties set out to find him.

The searchers found that Franklin's ships had been frozen in the ice and Franklin and 24 crew members had died of hunger, cold and disease. In 1848, the remaining 105 crew had left the ships and set out for Fort Resolution, the nearest settlement. None arrived.

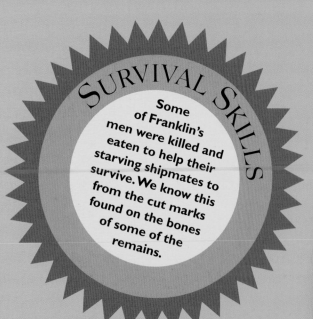

## SURVIVAL SKILLS

Some of Franklin's men were killed and eaten to help their starving shipmates to survive. We know this from the cut marks found on the bones of some of the remains.

Name: John Franklin
Born: 15 April, 1786, Spilsby, England
Died: 11 June, 1847, near King William Island, northern Canada
Notable achievements: Franklin's expedition failed to navigate the Northwest Passage, but did prove that it existed. His two ships, the *Erebus* and the *Terror*, successfully picked their way through the maze of islands known today as the District of Franklin. In May 1847, Franklin's party also found a route through the Victoria and Simpson Straits. Although all the crew perished, a record of the expedition's discovery of the passage was found in 1859.

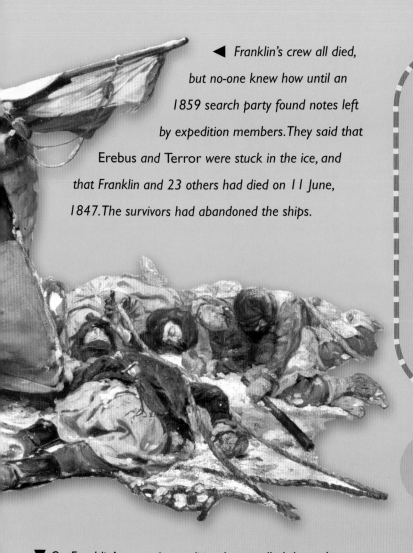

◄ *Franklin's crew all died, but no-one knew how until an 1859 search party found notes left by expedition members. They said that Erebus and Terror were stuck in the ice, and that Franklin and 23 others had died on 11 June, 1847. The survivors had abandoned the ships.*

## LONG TIME COMING

From the 16th century onwards, explorers had searched in vain for the Northwest Passage as a short-cut to Asia. Vitus Bering and Franklin proved such a route existed, but Norwegian explorer Roald Amundsen was the first to sail through it in 1903–1906, in his ship the Gjøa. The first merchant ship to cross the passage was the ice-breaker Manhattan in 1969, 400 years after the first explorers went there!

Franklin noted that the Arctic was so cold, his tea froze seconds after it was poured.

▼ *On Franklin's second expedition he travelled down the Mackenzie River to the Arctic coast. Franklin confirmed that Alexander Mackenzie's 1789 survey of what was then called the Great River was accurate, and renamed the river in Mackenzie's honour.*

As food ran out, the men survived by eating lichen and maggots in rotting deerskins!

# PEARY AND HENSON

AMERICAN ROBERT E. PEARY WAS
DETERMINED TO BE THE FIRST
PERSON TO REACH THE NORTH
POLE. MANY HAD TRIED; PEARY HAD
ALREADY FAILED SIX TIMES HIMSELF.

In his 50s, Peary made one last attempt, leading a
party of 24 men and 133 dogs. There were soon
problems – two sledges broke on the first day,
then two men got lost in a blizzard. Despite the
freezing temperatures, Peary drove his team on.

In March 1909, Peary made a final push for
the Pole, accompanied by Matthew Henson and
four Inuit men. They finally reached the Pole on
6 April. Peary spent 24 hours making sure he was
in the right place, then headed south again. No-one
else reached the Pole on foot for another 60 years!

▼ Peary used four experienced Inuits as dog-drivers.
In just five days they managed to cover 250 km
(155 miles) in extreme conditions where temperatures
were often below -30°C (-85°F).

LOOK CLOSER

Peary
combined old
and new survival
methods. He built igloos
and wore furs like the
Inuit. He also invented
a system of travelling
that used support
teams and supply
dumps.

◀ Although Peary wore furs, his legs were frostbitten up to
the knees. The tips of his toes came away with his shoes!

Name: Robert Edwin Peary
Born: 6 May, 1856, Cresson, Pa., U.S.
Died: 20 February, 1920,
Washington, D.C., U.S.

Name: Matthew Alexander Henson
Born: 8 August, 1866, Md., U.S.
Died: 9 March, 1955, NY, U.S.
Notable achievements: Commander Peary, his partner Henson and four Inuit men – Oatah, Egingwah, Ookeah and Seegloo – were credited as the first people to reach the North Pole, despite his rival Dr Frederick Cook claiming he had reached it first. It was Peary and Henson's eighth attempt to reach the Pole after almost 20 years of exploring the Arctic. From 1891 to 1895, they had made several expeditions to Greenland, confirming it was an island and bringing home three giant meteorites.

## WHO GOT THERE FIRST?

Matthew Henson probably beat Peary to the North Pole by 45 minutes. The African American had travelled with Peary since they met in a hat store in 1888. The explorer hired Henson as a valet on an expedition to Nicaragua. Impressed by Henson's skill as a navigator, Peary later took him on seven trips to the Arctic. Henson also proved a talented sled-driver in the Arctic terrain, and helped to keep good relations with the Inuit.

▶ Henson learned to translate between Peary and the Inuit.

# AMUNDSEN AND SCOTT

W HEN ROBERT PEARY REACHED THE NORTH POLE, EXPLORERS' EYES TURNED TO THE SOUTH POLE. TWO RIVAL EXPEDITIONS SET OFF, ONE LED BY ENGLISH NAVAL OFFICER ROBERT SCOTT, AND THE OTHER BY ROALD AMUNDSEN, A NORWEGIAN EXPLORER.

Scott was not expecting a race. He thought Amundsen was planning an expedition to the North Pole. Amundsen only told Scott (and his own men) of his change of plans when he was halfway across the Atlantic. In 1911, when both teams arrived in the Antarctic, they created supply depots for the route back, then spent the winter in huts.

On 19 October, at the beginning of the Antarctic summer, Amundsen's party set off. It travelled quickly across the ice and was lucky to find a pass through the Trans-Antarctic Mountains. Despite blizzards and a narrow escape from the crevasses of the 'Devil's Ballroom', Amundsen's team reached the South Pole on 14 December, 1911.

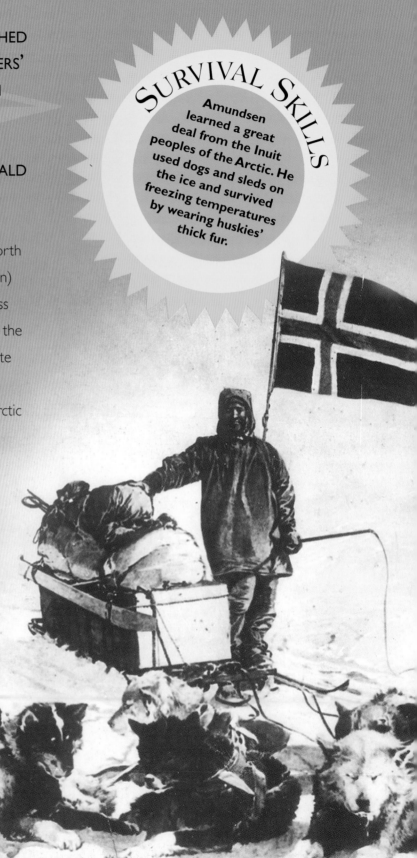

**SURVIVAL SKILLS**

Amundsen learned a great deal from the Inuit peoples of the Arctic. He used dogs and sleds on the ice and survived freezing temperatures by wearing huskies' thick fur.

▶ Amundsen (pictured at the South Pole with the Norwegian flag) and his five-man team trekked to the Pole and back to their base – a distance of 3,000 km (1,865 miles) – in just 99 days.

Name: Roald Engelbregt Amundsen

Born: 16 July, 1872, Borge, Norway

Died: c. 18 June, 1928, Arctic

Notable achievements: In 1911, Amundsen led the first expedition to reach the South Pole. He had dreamed of being a polar explorer all his life, but first made a name for himself from 1903 to 1906. With a crew of six aboard the ship Gjøa, he successfully navigated the Northwest Passage. During the same voyage he also became the first explorer to find the magnetic North Pole. In the 1920s, Amundsen explored the Arctic extensively by air and was part of the first team to fly over the North Pole. However, he vanished in June 1928 when his plane crashed on a mission to rescue other explorers stuck in the Arctic.

▲ Amundsen's team sped across the ice using skis and sleds pulled by huskies. These tough dogs could also be used as food when supplies ran low. Amundsen killed 22 dogs to provide meat for the return journey.

## SLOW PROGRESS

Scott and Amundsen were both helped by Fridtjof Nansen (1861–1930), the 'father of Polar exploring'. When Nansen's ship, the Fram, got caught in pack ice off the coast of Siberia, he let it drift for three years. He used dogs and sleds to travel to within 320 km (199 miles) of the North Pole – farther north than anyone had reached before.

▶ The Fram was specially designed to resist being crushed by the ice.

When Amundsen reached the Pole, Scott was still 580 km (360 miles) behind. His five-man team hauled their sledges up the Beardmore Glacier and across the high polar plateau. After 81 gruelling days, Scott reached the South Pole – and found the Norwegian flag and messages left by Amundsen. Devastated that they had lost the race, Scott's men turned for home.

Already worn out by their trek, Scott's team was hit by freak extreme weather: endless blizzards and temperatures well below average. 'Taff' Evans died from the extreme cold after he got injured in a fall. Lawrence 'Titus' Oates walked out into a blizzard and was never seen again. Scott and his surviving colleagues, Henry Bowers and Edward Wilson, were trapped in their tent for eight days by a blizzard. They died there when they became too weak from hunger to carry on. They were only 18 km (11 miles) from their supply base. Amundsen had won the race to the Pole, but Scott's bravery made him a hero.

Scott wrote his diary of the expedition even when he knew he would not survive.

He wrote: 'We are getting weaker, of course, and the end cannot be far.'

The last entry read: 'It seems a pity, but I do not think I can write more.'

Name: Robert Falcon Scott
Born: 6 June, 1868, Devonport, England
Died: 29 March, 1912, Antarctica
Notable achievement: Captain Scott and his men are remembered for their courage in losing the race to the South Pole. Scott had no Polar experience when he was asked to lead an expedition to Antarctica from 1901 to 1904. However, his team got within 725 km (450 miles) of the South Pole before having to turn back. In June 1910 Scott set off to Antarctica again on the ship the *Terra Nova* and reached the South Pole on 18 January, 1912, a month after Amundsen. Scott's gripping diary of the heroic journey was later published and became a best-seller.

◀ *Scott and his companions reached the South Pole – only to find the Norwegian flag and the tent where Amundsen and his men had spent three days while they took scientific measurements of the weather conditions.*

## LOOK CLOSER

On 12 November, 1912, a search party found the frozen bodies of Scott, Bowers and Wilson in a collapsed tent, together with Scott's diaries and valuable scientific records.

▼ *When the search party found Scott's body, they also found his diary and geological specimens the expedition had collected. Before they left, the search party erected a cairn in honour of the dead explorers.*

## LEGENDARY BRAVERY

The bravery of one of Scott's team has become particularly famous. Captain Oates' legs and feet were badly frostbitten, making it hard for him to keep up. He knew he was slowing down the others and putting their lives in danger. Time was running out. The men were suffering from scurvy and snowblindness, and their fuel containers were leaking. On the morning of 17 March, 1912, Oates stepped out of the tent into a blizzard. He was deliberately sacrificing himself to save the others. His final words were 'I am just going outside and may be some time.'

It was his 32nd birthday.

# DOUGLAS MAWSON

**D**OUGLAS MAWSON WAS AN AUSTRALIAN SCIENTIST WHO HAD EXPLORED ISLANDS IN THE PACIFIC. IN 1907 HE SWAPPED COCONUT TREES FOR BLIZZARDS WHEN HE JOINED ERNEST SHACKLETON'S EXPEDITION TO ANTARCTICA.

Four years later, Mawson led an expedition to map the Antarctic coastline. Sailing 1,500 km (932 miles) through pack ice, his ship the *Aurora* arrived on the Antarctic coastline in January 1912. After spending a stormy winter at Cape Denison, the expedition split into three groups. Mawson set off east with Dr Xavier Mertz, Lieutenant Belgrave Ninnis and 17 dogs.

They faced appalling weather and difficult terrain. When Mertz and Ninnis died, Mawson was alone and without supplies. Incredibly, travelling 160 km (99 miles) through howling gales and over deep crevasses, he made it back to base – to find that the *Aurora* had just left! Five men had stayed behind to look for him, however. Mawson and they spent a second winter in the Antarctic before they were rescued.

Name: Douglas Mawson
Born: 5 May, 1882, Shipley, England
Died: 14 October, 1958, Adelaide, Australia
Notable achievements: Mawson was one of the first scientists to explore the continent of Antarctica. Together with T.W.E David, he travelled 2,000 km (1,243 miles) to reach the Magnetic South Pole. From 1911 to 1914 he led an Australasian Antarctic expedition that explored some 3,000 km (1,865 miles) of undiscovered Antarctic coastline. From 1929 to 1931 Mawson led a joint British, Australian and New Zealand expedition to Antarctica, mapping another 4,000 km (2,486 miles) of previously little-known coastline.

Mawson claimed that the Cape Denison base was the windiest place on Earth.

He titled his book about the 1911-1914 expedition "The Home of the Blizzard".

LOOK CLOSER

Mawson and Mertz were forced to eat their huskies to survive. They ate everything. Unfortunately, Vitamin A in the dogs' livers poisoned the two explorers.

▲ Mawson was a large man and was incredibly fit and tough. He was known for his ability to withstand extreme cold.

▼ During Ernest Shackleton's expedition to Antarctica from 1907 to 1909, Mawson was part of the first team to climb Mount Erebus — an ice-covered volcano almost 3,500 m (11,482 ft) high.

## FIGHT WITH DEATH

Five weeks into their trek, Ninnis fell into a deep crevasse, together with most of the food. Mawson and Mertz decided to head back to base camp. Mawson later wrote, 'it was to be a fight with death'. When Mertz also died, Mawson went on alone. He too fell into a crevasse and was only saved when his sledge got wedged in the ice above. Although Mawson was tempted to cut the rope that held him, a voice inside him told him not to give up.

# ERNEST SHACKLETON

ERNEST SHACKLETON INSPIRED REMARKABLE TRUST AMONG HIS MEN. HE LED AN ATTEMPT TO CROSS THE ANTARCTIC ON FOOT.

By January 1915, Shackleton's ship the *Endurance* was trapped in pack ice. After drifting for 10 months, it was slowly crushed and eventually sank. With no hope of being rescued, Shackleton led his men 290 km (180 miles) to the solid rock of Elephant Island. From here, he and five others set off for South Georgia, an island 1,300 km (808 miles) away across the world's coldest and roughest ocean.

Incredibly, they made it in 16 days. Shackleton then led two men across the icy, mountainous island to a whaling station on its north coast and started a rescue. Shackleton's men were right to trust him – his leadership saved all 27 of the crew.

## SURVIVAL SKILLS

Shackleton and two of his crew used frozen coils of rope to toboggan hundreds of metres down the steep sides of the huge 2,743 m (9,000 ft) mountains of South Georgia.

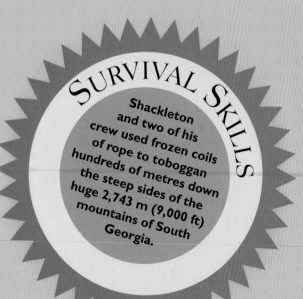

Name: Ernest Henry Shackleton
Born: 15 February, 1874, Kilkea, Ireland
Died: 5 January, 1922, South Georgia, South Atlantic Ocean
Notable achievements: Shackleton is best known for leading his crew to safety after *Endurance* was lost during a failed attempt to cross Antarctica on foot. Shackleton was already famous for the Nimrod expedition (1907 to 1909), during which he led a sledging party that came within 156 km (97 miles) of reaching the South Pole. Another party in the expedition, led by T.W.E. David, reached the Magnetic South Pole. Shackleton returned to England and was knighted as a hero.

◄ *Shackleton sailed across the South Atlantic in the* James Caird, *a lifeboat just 7 m (23 ft) long. As well as facing icebergs, gales and 20-m- (64-ft-) high waves, his crew had to chip away heavy ice that formed on the boat to stop it from sinking.*

> Shackleton was a born leader who could inspire brave men to follow him anywhere.

> The men left behind on Elephant Island survived by hunting penguins and seals.

> They lived under two upturned lifeboats as there was very little shelter on the island.

▼ *The* Endurance *sank when it was crushed by pack ice. Shackleton's men lived on the floating ice for four months before they reached Elephant Island.*

# ACROSS THE WORLD

### sea ● sea ● and yet more sea!

ONLY 500 YEARS AGO, PEOPLE FEARED THE SEAS WERE FULL OF STRANGE CREATURES SUCH AS MERMAIDS, MONSTERS AND GIANTS. A VOYAGE ACROSS THE OCEAN WAS A TRIP INTO A TERRIFYING WORLD.

# ACROSS THE WORLD

DESPITE THE HAZARDS, DURING THE 16TH CENTURY BRAVE SEAFARERS SUCH AS FERDINAND MAGELLAN AND FRANCIS DRAKE SAILED AROUND THE WORLD IN TINY SHIPS USING ONLY VERY BASIC NAVIGATION.

Today, the planet seems much smaller. Satellites beam down pictures of every inch of the planet's surface. There are few places humans have not been: in 1952 Tenzing Norgay and Sir Edmund Hillary climbed Mount Everest, the highest mountain, and in 1960 Jacques Piccard plunged to the deepest part of the ocean, the Mariana Trench.

Even before the exploration of Earth was finished, people began to explore a new frontier: space. We have come a long way from early humans spreading across the planet in search of food, but we still look out into space and wonder, 'What is out there?'

## WHY GO THERE?

- **TRADE:** *Mariners were usually looking for short-cuts to places like the Spice Islands, that were useful for trade.*
- **PIRACY:** *Francis Drake sailed around the world to attack Spanish ships in the Pacific and steal any gold they were carrying.*
- **CURIOSITY:** *Some Europeans thought people on the far side of the planet must live upside down, with feet on their heads!*

## KEY

→ *Magellan*

⇢ *Magellan's ships*

→ *Drake*

● *Places of interest*

▲ *Francis Drake was knighted by Queen Elizabeth I for sailing around the world in the 1570s.*

◄ *Dame Ellen McArthur set a record for non-stop sailing around the world in 2005: 71 days, 14 hours.*

NORTH AMERICA

*ATLANTIC OCEAN*

**Plymouth** ●  EUROPE

● **Seville**

Death of Magellan

Marianas

ASIA

CAPE VERDE ISLANDS

AFRICA

*INDIAN OCEAN*

SPICE ISLANDS

**Port Guatulco** ●

SOUTH AMERICA

**Lima** ●

*PACIFIC OCEAN*

**Rio de Janeiro**

OCEANIA

**Valparaiso** ●

*River Plate*

*PACIFIC OCEAN*

**San Julián**

*STRAITS OF MAGELLAN*

Tierra del Fuego

CAPE OF GOOD HOPE

*Borders and some modern day country names are not shown*

1500 km (932 miles)

ANTARCTICA

# FERDINAND MAGELLAN

**A**LTHOUGH FEW PEOPLE BELIEVED HIM, SEA CAPTAIN FERDINAND MAGELLAN INSISTED HE COULD REACH EAST ASIA BY SAILING WEST.

In September 1519, Magellan set sail from Seville in Spain with five tiny ships and 280 men. The voyage was fraught with hardship and mutiny. In March 1520, one ship was wrecked in a gale. In October, another turned back, taking most of the fleet's supplies.

Magellan crossed the 'Sea of the South', which he named the Pacific Ocean, in four months. He reached Guam, then sailed to the Philippines. Here Magellan got involved in a local war and was killed. However, two of his ships reached the Moluccas, and one, the *Victoria*, continued west. It reached Spain on 6 September, 1522, becoming the first ship to sail around the world.

Name: Ferdinand Magellan
Born: 1480, Oporto, Portugal
Died: 1521, Mactan, Philippines
Notable achievement:
Ferdinand Magellan charted one of the greatest feats of navigation in history. Intending to reach the Spice Islands by sailing west around South America, he succeeded in reaching and then sailing across the Pacific Ocean. Although killed in the Philippines, he had made it around the world by overlapping one of his earlier courses, where he had sailed east to the South China Seas and passed the Philippines.

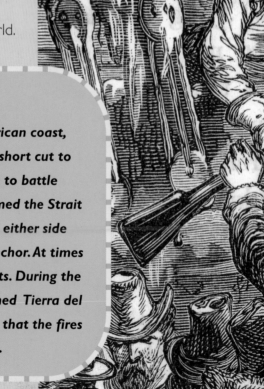

## STRAIT OF MAGELLAN

**I**n October 1520, sailing along the South American coast, Magellan sighted what he hoped would be a short cut to the Pacific Ocean. In fact, it took over a month to battle through the 580-km (360-mile) strait (later named the Strait of Magellan). Snow-capped mountains loomed either side and the rocky bottom made it impossible to anchor. At times Magellan had to tow his ships with rowing boats. During the trip he saw many fires on islands which he named Tierra del Fuego or 'Land of Fires'. Magellan was terrified that the fires were lit by tribes waiting to ambush his fleet.

▶ Only one of Magellan's five ships and just 18 of his men survived the 'round the world' trip. Captained by Sebastian del Cano, The Victoria, a replica of which is shown here, completed the voyage in just over three years.

> The Guarani Indians in Brazil believed Magellan was a god and showered him with gifts.

> In the Mariana Islands, his crew met warriors with shields decorated with human hair!

## SURVIVAL SKILLS

Magellan's Spanish captains did not like taking orders from a Portuguese man. When they mutinied, Magellan executed the leaders and marooned an officer on the South American coast.

◀ On 2 April, 1520, a mutiny broke out involving two of the five ships' captains. However, it was unsuccessful because the crews remained loyal to Magellan.

# FUTURE
# FRONTIERS

planets ● outer space ●
deep ocean

# OCEANS

UNTIL THE LATE TWENTIETH CENTURY, A JOURNEY TO THE BOTTOM OF THE SEA WAS JUST A FANTASY. BUT ON 23 JANUARY, 1960, JACQUES PICCARD AND DONALD WALSH REACHED THE OCEAN FLOOR IN *TRIESTE*.

The 10,916-m (35,800-ft) descent to 'Challenger Deep' in the Mariana Trench off the Philippines took almost five hours. The two men spent just twenty minutes on the ocean floor, but are still the only people to have reached the deepest part of any ocean on Earth.

Then, in 1977, the three-man submersible *Alvin* discovered hot springs over 2.5 km (1.5 miles) deep off the coast of Equador, along with sea creatures such as giant tube worms and huge clams. Who knows what else lurks in the deepest parts of the oceans?

## SURVIVAL SKILLS

*Trieste* had a gas-filled float chamber for buoyancy and a separate sphere for the crew. The sphere's walls were 12.7 cm (5 in) thick to withstand water pressure on the seabed.

◀ *The discovery of the unusual creatures that live in permanent darkness at the bottom of the ocean changed our understanding of life on Earth. It proved that life could survive without light energy from the Sun.*

Around 1624 Cornelius van Drebel, a Dutch inventor, tested the first submarine.

In 1958 USS *Nautilus* made the first submerged voyage under the Arctic ice pack.

◀ The deep-sea submersible Deep Rover can carry a crew of two to depths of 1,000 m (3,280 ft). It can also tow equipment, such as platforms used in underwater construction.

## DEEP-SEA DIVER

Sylvia Earle is an undersea explorer and marine biologist. In 60 expeditions and over 7,000 hours of underwater exploration, she has discovered many new species and set many diving records, including a dive 385 m (1,260 ft) down to the ocean floor off Hawaii. She descended while strapped to a submarine, then walked around the bottom wearing an armoured diving suit to protect her against the incredible water pressure.

▶ The Self Contained Underwater Breathing Apparatus, or SCUBA, supplies oxygen to divers and allows them to stay underwater for several hours.

# SPACE

On 20 July, 1969, US Astronaut Neil Armstrong became the first person to set foot on the Moon. He made the memorable comment, 'That's one small step for [a] man, one giant leap for mankind'.

The three-man Apollo mission had blasted off from Florida three days earlier. Armstrong and Buzz Aldrin guided the Lunar Module down to the Moon's surface and spent around 21 hours there.

After World War II, the 'Space Race' between the Soviet Union and the USA led to the launch of satellites in the 1950s. In 1961, Soviet cosmonaut Yuri Gagarin became the first person in space. Since the 1980s, the rival space agencies have co-operated, resulting in the International Space Station, and most astronauts have travelled into space on board reusable space shuttles.

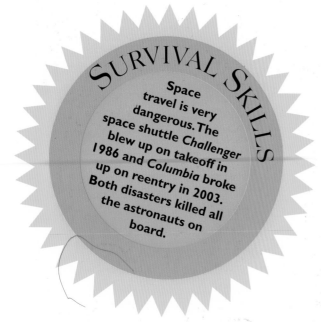

SURVIVAL SKILLS

Space travel is very dangerous. The space shuttle Challenger blew up on takeoff in 1986 and Columbia broke up on reentry in 2003. Both disasters killed all the astronauts on board.

▲ The Apollo space programme was the most ambitious project of the 20th century. Launched by the powerful three-stage Saturn V rocket, there were 17 missions in all, six of which took crews to the surface of the Moon.

## ROBOTS ON MARS

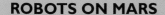

Human explorers are being replaced by robots in outer space. In 1975, two Viking probes landed on the surface of the planet Mars to collect data. Then, in January 2004, the robots **Spirit** and **Opportunity** landed on opposite sides of the 'Red Planet'. They are still going strong, having covered many kilometres of the planet. The salty soil they have found suggests that Mars once had enough water to support life! In future, a mobile science lab may be sent to Mars, along with robots that will burrow and drill for underground water supplies.

▼ Opportunity examines Martian rocks and other features on the planet's surface and transmits the data back to Earth.

▲ The space shuttle, photographed above the Earth by a camera attached to its robotic arm, is designed to be used a number of times. Earlier rockets could only be launched once, making space travel very expensive.

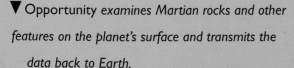

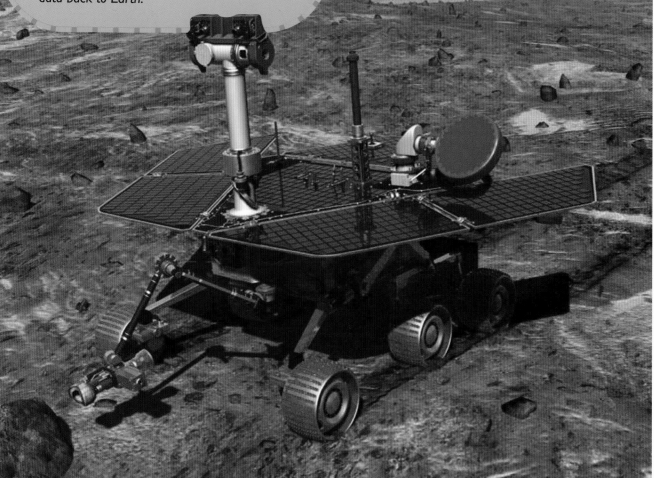

# BRITISH AND IRISH EXPLORERS

The explorers in this book are just some of the adventurers who have set out to discover new lands. Britain and Ireland have a tradition of exploration that includes 16th-century mariners who sailed the Atlantic, and pioneers who visited Africa and Australia in the 18th and 19th centuries. They helped the British create the largest empire the world has ever seen. Other explorers were missionaries spreading religion, or scientists searching for new plants and animals. Here are some interesting individuals – their adventures might make you pleased you stayed at home!

**THOMAS ATKINSON (1799-1861)** was an English artist who, with his wife Lucy, spent the years around 1850 painting watercolours as they travelled nearly 40,000 miles through parts of eastern Russia and Central Asia that few Europeans had visited. Lucy spent part of the trip caring for her baby son, who was born near Russia's border with China.

**WILLIAM BAFFIN (C. 1584-1622)** was an English mariner who in 1616 discovered Baffin Island and Baffin Bay near northwest Greenland as he searched for a sea route to Asia. Over 300 years later, modern explorers confirmed that one of the bays Baffin explored really was the start of a Northwest Passage that led to Asia.

**JOHN CABOT (C.1450-1499)** was born in Italy but moved to England in 1495. Sponsored by King Henry VII of England, Cabot sailed to Canada in 1497 in a small ship, the *Matthew*. He landed near Labrador, Newfoundland, on June 24, 1497, and became the first European to reach North America after the Vikings.

**TOM CREAN (1877-1938)** was an Irish explorer who made two polar journeys with Robert F. Scott. On the 1911–1913 *Terra Nova* expedition to the South Pole, Crean's bravery in saving the lives of Teddy Evans and William Lashly earned him the Albert Medal. On Ernest Shackleton's *Endurance* expedition (1914–1916), Crean was one of the six men who braved the stormy Atlantic seas in an open boat, sailing to South Georgia to get help.

**WILLIAM DAMPIER (C.1652-1715)** was an English explorer and mapmaker – and part-time pirate! Working for the British Navy, Dampier sailed to Australia and around the South Pacific, charting coastlines, rivers and currents. He kept detailed notes of his voyages (including the first written record of a typhoon) that he later turned into a best-selling book, *A New Voyage Around the World* (1697).

**CHARLES DARWIN (1809-1882)** was an English scientist who went on a five-year around-the-world voyage in HMS *Beagle* to study plants and animals. Darwin wrote down everything he saw in a journal, which later helped him to write his book *On the Origin of Species* (1859), which changed forever how people thought about living things.

**SIR FRANCIS DRAKE (1543-1596)** was an English explorer and pirate. In his ship the *Golden Hind*, Drake led the second expedition to sail around the world (1577–1580), crossing the Atlantic, Indian and Pacific oceans. On his return home, he was knighted by a delighted Queen Elizabeth I: his ship was laden with silver, looted from Spanish ships and settlements on the way.

**EDWARD JOHN EYRE (1815-1901)** together with his aboriginal friend Wylie, was the first man to cross southern Australia from east to west, travelling across the Nullarbor Plain from Adelaide to Albany. During the tough 4½ month trek, the two men were forced to eat kangaroos and even a dead penguin to stay alive!

**SIR RANULPH FIENNES (1944- )** described by the *Guinness Book of Records* as the 'world's greatest living explorer', has led more than 30 expeditions to the Poles, across deserts and to many other remote places. In 1992, Fiennes and others found the legendary Lost City of Ubar, known as 'the Atlantis of the Sands', in the desert of Oman. A year later, he and Mike Stroud walked across Antarctica, each pulling a 225-kg sledge.

SIR MARTIN FROBISHER
(1535?-1594)
was a former pirate who made three voyages to north-eastern North America to search for a Northwest Passage. None were successful. On this third voyage, Frobisher dug several gold mines, only to find on his return home that the rocks he had dug up were worthless!

WILLIAM HILTON HOVELL
(1786-1875)
along with Australian explorer Hamilton Hume, was the first European to cross south-eastern Australia between what are now Sydney and Melbourne.

HENRY HUDSON (1565-1611)
was an English explorer and navigator who explored north-eastern North America and parts of the Arctic Ocean. Like many others, he was searching for a quick route to Asia from Europe. The Hudson River, Hudson Strait and Hudson Bay are all named after him. When Hudson and his son argued with their crew, they set them both adrift in a small boat – never to be heard of again.

JOHN OXLEY (1785-1828)
was an English explorer who mapped large areas of eastern Australia and Tasmania, including the Lachlan River region, the Macquarie River and Moreton Bay. After bumping into two escaped convicts who were living with the local aborigines, he learned of a nearby 'big river' – the Brisbane River, which he found in 1824.

JOHN RAE (1813-1893)
was a Scottish explorer, surveyor and surgeon who explored the Canadian Arctic. Rae surveyed and mapped over 1,400 miles (2255 km) of uncharted Canadian coastline. He also made three voyages to find Sir John Franklin: on his third journey, he learned from local Inuit how Franklin had died.

SIR WALTER RALEIGH (1554-1618)
was an English poet, historian and soldier as well as explorer. He organized several expeditions to North America and built a colony on the east coast of North America that he named Virginia. He also led an expedition to Guiana on the north coast of South America in search of 'El Dorado', the fabled land of gold.

JOHN ROSS (1777-1856)
was a Scottish naval officer who twice tried to find a Northwest Passage to Asia in the icy seas west of Greenland. In 1829 his converted paddle-steamer became stuck in the ice, and Ross and his crew waited four years for rescue. They lived off food stores from an old shipwreck. While they were waiting, Ross's nephew James Clark Ross made a number of overland expeditions – on one of which he discovered the magnetic North Pole.

ALEXANDER SELKIRK (1676-1721)
was a Scottish sailor who argued with his captain and was abandoned on a tiny Pacific island 400 miles from the coast of Chile. He survived on his own for four years before being rescued – by then, he had forgotten how to speak! When Selkirk returned to Britain, his story became the basis for the classic book *Robinson Crusoe* by Daniel Defoe.

HESTER LUCY STANHOPE
(LADY STANHOPE) (1776-1839)
was an English aristocrat who moved to the Middle East after her lover and brother both died fighting the French in 1809. At a time when few Europeans visited the Middle East – especially women – she travelled through the Holy Land disguised as an Arab man. In Syria she lived with Bedouin nomads who called her 'the Queen of the Desert'. She spent the last decades of her life in an old monastery she bought in Lebanon.

FREYA STARK (1893-1993)
was a British traveller who in the middle of the 20th century became the first European woman to visit many remote areas of Turkey and the Middle East, although her travels took her as far as Afghanistan and Nepal. She wrote many books about her journeys.

DAVID THOMPSON (1770-1857)
was a Welsh explorer, mapmaker and fur trader. He explored western North America and was the first person to make detailed maps of the region. In 1807, Thompson crossed the Rocky Mountains and became the first European to travel the entire length of the Columbia River.

JAMES WEDDELL (1787-1834)
was an English explorer and scientist who sailed on three expeditions to the Antarctic. In 1823 he also sailed closer to the South Pole than anyone else for the next 80 years. He also discovered the Weddell Sea (near the South Pole) and the Weddell Seal, both named after him.

# GLOSSARY

■ **ANTARCTICA**
The fifth largest continent, a mass of land around the South Pole covered by an ice cap over 2 km thick.

■ **ARCTIC**
The frozen ocean around the North Pole. It is a giant sheet of floating ice ringed by land – the northern coasts of Russia, Alaska, Canada and Greenland.

■ **ASTRONAUT**
Someone who travels into space.

■ **AUSTRALIAN ABORIGINES**
The people who lived in Australia before the Europeans arrived. About 400,000 of their descendents live in Australia today.

■ **CANNIBAL**
A person who eats the bodies of other people.

■ **CARGO**
Goods carried on a ship or plane.

■ **COLONY**
A settlement of people who leave their country to go to live in a new land.

■ **COMPASS**
An instrument, usually with a magnetic needle, that points north and allows travellers to work out their position.

■ **CREVASSE**
Deep cracks (some over 30 m deep) that form in a glacier when it moves.

■ **EMPIRE**
A large territory made up of many different countries all ruled by one person or state.

■ **EQUATOR**
An imaginary line around the Earth at its widest point which divides the Northern and Southern Hemispheres.

■ **EXPEDITION**
A voyage made for a particular reason.

■ **FRONTIER**
The wilderness at the edge of a settled area.

■ **GLACIER**
A large river of ice that moves slowly downhill.

■ **GREAT SOUTHERN CONTINENT**
A legendary land mass in the South Seas which explorers thought existed up until the late 18th century.

■ **HIMALAYAS**
A mountain range stretching 2,400 km across India and Tibet. It contains the world's highest mountain, Mount Everest.

■ **INUIT**
One of the native peoples of the Arctic, the Inuits live in Canada, Greenland and Alaska. They were once known as Eskimos.

■ **MAGNETIC POLE**
The points on the Earth's surface where the Earth's magnetic field is strongest. Though they are always close to the geographical North and South poles, the magnetic poles constantly move in a circle about 160 km wide.

■ **MALARIA**
A dangerous disease spread among humans by mosquito bites.

■ **MARINER**
Someone who travels by sea.

■ **MIDDLE EAST**
A large area of southwest Asia and North Africa east of the Mediterranean Sea and west of Pakistan, which includes the Arabian Peninsula.

■ **MIGRATION**
A journey by a large group of people moving to a new place to live.

■ **MISSIONARY**
Someone who travels to another country to convert people to his or her religion.

■ **MONGOLS**
A group of peoples from East Central Asia whose leader Genghis Khan created an empire stretching from China to Persia in the 13th century.

■ **NATIVE AMERICANS**
The people who lived in North, Central and South America before the arrival of European explorers and settlers.

■ **NAVIGATOR**
Someone who is skilled at setting a course for a ship.

■ **THE NEW WORLD**
The name Europeans gave to North, Central and South America when they discovered them in the 15th and 16th centuries.

■ **NORTHWEST PASSAGE**
A sea route from the Atlantic to the Pacific Ocean through the Arctic waters north of Canada and Alaska.

■ **OASIS**
A place in the desert where plants can grow because

of water that rises from underground rocks.

■ **PILGRIM**

Someone who travels to other countries to visit holy sites.

■ **PIONEER**

One of the first people to explore or settle in a new land (though native people may already be living there).

■ **PORTER**

Someone who carries luggage or equipment on an expedition.

■ **RAPIDS**

A fast-flowing and often dangerous part of a river.

■ **REEF**

A ridge of coral or rock just above or below the surface of the sea.

■ **SCURVY**

A dangerous disease caused by lack of vitamin C.

■ **SILK ROAD**

A network of overland trade routes across Asia linking Europe, China, and India and used by merchants since ancient times.

■ **SOUTH SEAS**

The southern Pacific Ocean.

■ **SOURCE**

The beginning of a river.

■ **SPICE**

A flavouring such as nutmeg or cloves that is used to change the taste of food or to disguise the taste of stale food.

■ **SPICE ISLANDS**

The old name for the Moluccas, famous for their spices and now part of Indonesia.

■ **STRAIT**

A narrow channel of water that joins two much larger areas of water. For example, the Straits of Magellan link the Atlantic and Pacific oceans at the southern tip of South America.

■ **SURVEY**

To make a map of somewhere.

■ **TROPICS**

A broad band lying between two imaginary lines around the Earth on either side of the Equator where the climate is generally warm.

■ **TYPHOID**

A dangerous disease caused by drinking dirty water.

# FURTHER READING

## THE TIMES ATLAS OF WORLD EXPLORATION
by Glyn Williams and Felipe Fernandez-Armesto (HarperReference, 1991)

## PATHFINDERS: A GLOBAL HISTORY OF EXPLORATION
by Felipe Fernandez-Armesto (OUP, 2007)

## THE FABER BOOK OF EXPLORATION
by Benedict Allen (Faber and Faber, 2004)

## ATLAS OF EXPLORATION
by Shona Grimbly (Fitzroy Dearborn, 2001)

## THE SEVENTY GREAT JOURNEYS IN HISTORY
by Robin Hanbury-Tenison (Thames and Hudson, 2006)

# WEBSITES

*Ask an adult to help you find additional websites and check them out before you use them.*

Mariners' Museum Age of Exploration website:
*http://www.mariner.org/educationalad/ageofex/*

Library of Congress Learning Page on exploration and explorers:
*http://memory.loc.gov/learn/community/cc_exploration.php*

The Museum of Unnatural Mystery has a collection of stories in its Virtual Exploration Society:
*http://unmuseum.mus.pa.us/ves.htm*

Directory of highly readable articles about explorers and exploration:
*http://www.kidsolr.com/history/page2.html*

Collection of articles on Discoverers Web:
*http://www.win.tue.nl/%7Eengels/discovery/*

# INDEX

# ACKNOWLEDGEMENTS

**AKG Images:** 9t, 24, 34, 84b, 87b, 98/99; Vilstein Bild 102; **Alamy:** Winston Fraser 99; Jon Arnold Images Ltd 54/55; Ron Niebrugge 81b; North Wind Pictures 97t; Panorama Media (Beijing) Ltd 44/45; Photodisc 28/29; Robert Harding Picture Library Ltd 80; Eitan Simanor 38; **Ancient Art and Architecture Collection:** 40/41; Prisma 88; **Ardea:** Duncan Usher 44; **Art Archive:** 21t, 58; British Library 66b, 68; Gianni Dagli 83t; Musee des Arts Africains et Oceaniens/Gianni Dagli Orti 18t; Naval Museum, Madrid/Alfredo Dagli Orti 69t; Mireille Vautier 87t; **Bridgeman Art Library:** 77; Mitchell Library, State Library of New South Wales 55t; The British Museum 10; Corbis: 67b; Bettmann 11, 119; Leonard De Selva 23t; Julio Donoso 70; Phillipe Giraud/Goodlook 26/27; Jon Hicks 43; Stephen Hira/Reuters 6; Dave G. Houser 61; Hulton-Deutsch Collection 21tl; Joshua Jebb 74; Layne Kennedy 100/101; Jaques Langeuin 96; Michael Nicholson 17; Kazayoshi Nomachi 36, 39t; Alfred Russell 4b, 78/79; Skyscan 90/91; Paul A Souders 4t, 58/59; Penny Tweedle 60; Underwood & Underwood 108/109; Ralph White 118; **Gertrude Bell Photographic Archive:** University of Newcastle Upon Tyne 47b; **Getty Images:** Chris Anderson/Aurora 66t; Wallace Kirkland 65t; Samanatha Sin/AFP 115; Time & Life Pictures 16/17t; Kobal: RKO 39b; Tri-Star 20; **Mary Evans Picture Library:** 7t, 35b, 37b, 57b, 57t, 103, 104t, 105, 113t, 114/115; Doutaz Beranger 7b; Interfoto Agentur 37t; **Matthew Flinders Electronic Archive:** 55b; **NASA:** 116/117, 120, 121b, 121t; **NHPA:** Nick Garbutt 25; **NOAA:** 118/119; **Photodisc:** 52; **Photolibrary:** 67t; Daniel Cox 81t; **Photos.com:** 84t; **Shutterstock:** Joel Blit 86; Norman Chan 40/41; Constain-Ciprian Hirlestaenu 92/93; Susan Flashman 15t; Scott A Franges 79b; Lena Grottling 110/111; Danile Gustavsson 51l; Efemova Irine 45; Mates Krajcovic 76/77; Mary Lane 75t; Ales Liska 83b; Johnny Lye 63/64; Mikhail Matsonashvil 69b; Max FX 79t; David McKee 19; Colin & Linda McKie 53; Jakob Metzger 5t, 12/13; Andre Nantel 15b; Daniel Pash 89; Dmitry Pichugin 21b; Styve Reineck 56/57; Ronald Sumners 48/49; Mike Von Bergern 88/89; Ke Wang 35t; Peter Zaharou 46; **Still Pictures:** 33, 51r 106/107; (Freelens Poll) Tack 72r; H. Brehm 22; Dani-Jeske 31r; Michael Sewell 95; **Superstock:** age/fotostock 18b; **Topham:** 27b , 27t, 31l, 47t, 52/53, 65b, 76, 79c, 91, 97b, 100, 103t, 106, 107, 108, 109, 113b, 114; Alinari 10/11, 16/17b; HIP 71r, 104b; HIP/British Library 42b, 42t; Photri 101; Print Collector/HIP 73, 90; Roger-Viollet 98; The Image Works 71l, 72l, 75b; World History Archive 23b, 32, 59, 61t; **Werner Forman:** 9b, 85b; N.J. Saunders 5b, 85t; **Wikimedia:** 41.

**GEOGRAPHY CONSULTANT:** CLIVE CARPENTER
**CHILDREN'S PUBLISHER:** ANNE O'DALY
**MANAGING EDITOR:** TIM COOKE
**EDITOR:** CLAIRE HAWCOCK
**DESIGNER:** STARRY DOGS
**DESIGN MANAGER:** SARAH WILLIAMS
**CREATIVE DIRECTOR:** JENI CHILD
**CARTOGRAPHER:** ALAN GILLILAND
**PICTURE RESEARCHER:** LAILA TORSUN